# The Ocotillo Review

**Volume 6.1**

**Winter 2022**

*The Ocotillo Review Volume 6.1*
©2022 Kallisto Gaia Press Inc.
All Rights Reserved



Attention schools and businesses: for discounted copies on large orders please contact the publisher dirctly.

Kallisto Gaia Press
1801 E. 51st Street
Suite 365-246
Austin TX. 78723
*info@kallistogaiapress.org*
(254) 654-7205

Cover art: **sayidat alzzyz** *(Cicada Lady)*
Organic sculpture under glass
**Michele Hernandez**

Edited by: Tony Burnett

**ISSN: 2573-4113**
**ISBN: 978-1-952224-20-1**

# The Ocotillo Review

**Volume 6.1**

**Winter 2022**

*FICTION - POETRY - TRUTH*

* - from our Summer Writing contests

^ - from our upcoming full-length poetry collections

Precious Readers,

For your enjoyment we offer to you this compilation of literary works from our neighbors on several continents. We have been semi-sequestered for almost two years as of this missive. Are we learning to adapt? Honestly, it's been strange, but seeing as disease and death are the alternatives, we have no other viable options. The Winter issue is always our largest and most diverse of the year. In this issue we traditionally share the winners of our Chester B. Himes Memorial Fiction Prize and the Julia Darling Memorial Poetry Prize. This year the entries were outstanding. It took an extra month to select the fiction finalists and an extra six weeks to select the poetry finalists. I want to thank our judges, May Cobb and Edward Vidaurre, who must have put in quite a few late evenings to get the results back in time to have this journal completed and in your hands right on schedule.

It's interesting to note that this issue took on its own theme organically. Our editorial team is set up so there's no communication between genres. Our poetry editor is in Illinois Our flash fiction editor is in St. Paul Minnesota, and although our nonfiction and short story editors live within a mile of each other here in Austin Texas, I'm not sure they've ever met. Yet as the editorial staff began to send their selections to me, I noted a theme of spirituality and religion forming. Frankly, I was terrified. Although I think of myself as a spiritual entity, that's very personal. I avoid organized religion as the dark side of the human experience. I would not want *The Ocotillo Review* to promote any religious doctrine any more than I would publish hate speech or pornography. So, we took most of the religion out and kept the spirituality. I'm going to attribute this anomaly to the social upheaval created by the virus. That virus can handle a bit more blame as far as I'm concerned.

This beefy little book includes some incredible writing. First, in addition to the contest winners we printed the runners-up. May Cobb also noted three honorable mentions in the short story prize. We published a couple of those. Later this year we will publish two full-length debut poetry collections. We are sharing a couple of poems from each of these. (Watch what I do here as I completely obliterate my earlier rant.)

The first collection is one from a San Antonio poet who has graced the pages of The Ocotillo Review in almost every issue. Charles Darnell has spent several years developing character arcs and understanding of both well-known and obscure inhabitants of one of the world's most translated, published, and controversial books.

Although these characters are from the Bible, I think you will find them to be as flawed, interesting, and human as anyone created by Mark Twain or Stephen King. Toward Human will publish in the fall. Look for preorders on our website.

The other poet was discovered by our new poetry editor, Tate Lewis-Carroll. Dan Smart has been published in a number of respected journals; he's written over 3000 poems since 2013; and his style reminds me of the late Tony Hoagland. How could I not take the opportunity to publish his first full-length collection? It will also debut in 2022, date and title to be announced.

It's my hope that we can get this virus under control or at least learn to coexist with it before we all die of skin hunger. I want to wish you a lovely season. I'm not going to ask you for a donation. We are all doing the best we can. If you're looking for something interesting to read, we are developing one heck of a catalogue.
Check it out.
Peace,


Tony

**Start Here.**

*It gets good!*

# ATOMIC FIELD

*Whether or not I listen, ghosts sob*
*on the atomic field.*
–Taniguchi Seinosuke

Turning inside your chest, an awakened heron.
A desire for eelgrass overcomes you.

At the top of the gingko, whose candleflame?
Crumbs of sleep rest at the bottom of a breath.

Draw on your flushed forehead a skeletal hand.
What the wind embraces the wind bends.

One moon, one swaying moon shadow.
Walk as if your legs were sea water in a plastic bag.

Speak so your voice lingers long in each pine needle.
Perhaps silence, the moon warns, will soothe you sore.

Wash the clotted numbers with sand and then ash.
Song, too, shall become you.

**- John Bradley**

# SYLVIE

TIMMY DIDN'T KNOW she was the pastor's daughter. He opened his eyes one night during praise and worship, and there she was. Long red hair, hand curled around the microphone. Tall. He recognized her from AA. When had she come on stage? She sang *Way Maker* with the team, and Timmy's heart pulsed into his fingertips. Her voice was an earthy, on-pitch alto.

You don't fall for someone in your meeting—Timmy hadn't. But inside Faith Church his love of the Spirit billowed into love for her. He felt excited and confused. Convicted. Her hand on the mic brought to mind a seashell. He knew her name. Sylvie.

When he was using and something churned him up inside, he'd have gone off with a couple fifths and some crystal. That would've taken care of him for days. He'd have been leveled and sexless when he came to himself again. This time, he had 113 days clean.

After the service he knew he should leave. He went to the front of the sanctuary instead. Up on stage Sylvie was talking with the other singer. Her freckled calves were eye level. Eventually she looked down.

Hi, Timmy said.

Sylvie said hi back. The look that passed between them was fear and understanding. Timmy's fingertips kept pulsing. He'd found a meeting outside Redham where no one would know him. Likely so had Sylvie.

The lights dimmed, and she walked offstage with the team. Timmy got in his pickup, drove home to his apartment.

He hated Faith Church, parts of it. He was there only because he couldn't not be. One night last winter, alone, he'd pulled into the parking lot. Inside, he meant to leave, but he sat down instead. People sang and prayed, cried. Timmy cried too. Afterwards he was sheepish and different.

That was three months ago. He'd kept going back. Something was there, call it the Holy Spirit, call it Jesus the radical who washed the feet of the poor. And Timmy had met some good people. But the fake holiness—men he knew sitting in the pews who misused their wives, women who didn't do right by their husbands and kids. The manager at Wendy's who'd fired Timmy when he was in rehab was an usher. Maybe Jesus would actually return and know what to do about how things were.

After he saw Sylvie, Timmy texted his sister, *Someone from my meeting at Faith tonight,* I like her, and Leah wrote back, *Go easy.*

Timmy understood— his meeting and what could happen if he and Sylvie started something that didn't go well. But he sidestepped that like he did now whenever the world's heaviness, or his own, pushed in. He lit candles, prayed for letting go. Put on early Linkin Park from when they were alternative. He made a pile of toast and went to bed carbed-out.

Sylvie didn't show up at AA on Friday. But Tuesday night she was back at Faith. She came out and joined the P&W team like before. *Break Every Chain*— she sang harmony. People around Timmy lifted their arms and swayed. So did he. He felt the Spirit through her, genuine. He was rebuilding a life from brokenness. Apparently so was she. The thought made him fractionally braver than last time. After the service he went to the stage and asked, Can I buy you coffee?
Yes, Sylvie said. Her cheeks and her lips were the same color.
Down in the carpeted atrium there was a line outside His Goodness. Timmy and Sylvie stood together quietly. He had so much to say, he could hardly say anything. Faith Church was nothing like the old steepled churches around Redham. Three stories, rows of theater-style seats in the sanctuary. Huge. Pastor Mac was in line behind them, laughing with some people. He always seemed happy, sometimes too much so. That kind of happiness could make another person's troubles weigh more. It did Timmy's.

Sylvie asked for cappuccino extra foam, he got a large coffee. They sat. Sun angled through the skylight and onto the floor. Timmy imagined Sylvie singing just for him. Imagined driving home with her in the passenger seat.
Then Pastor Mac came over. He leaned down and hugged her. Hello sweetie!
Hi, Dad.

Pastor's daughter in AA. So at least part of that cheerfulness was a front. Pastor Mac reached out to shake, his hand friendly yet firm. The look in his eyes said father-with-a-daughter. Timmy sat straighter, glad he'd worn a white shirt and blazer with his jeans, glad his missing teeth were molars. He wasn't what he'd been, but he still presented. He was twenty-seven.

After Pastor Mac moved on, Sylvie said, You didn't know he was my dad, and Timmy said he'd only started coming to Faith in January. She asked what he did, and he told her the journeyman program at JobWorks. Electronics. But he wanted to open a bakery.
It's what I'd really like to do. Timmy hadn't told anyone that before. He

was glad to have it out there for Sylvie, along with his AA self.

She'd grown up just outside Redham, homeschooled with other church kids, she said. Graduated college last May. She'd begun drinking her senior year. She sipped her coffee, licked foam from her lip. Said she'd come home from a missions trip to Bosnia last summer knowing she needed help. Timmy knew the rest from meetings: she'd quit drinking, cold, on New Years and joined AA. She had almost five months sober. The rest of her family didn't drink.

I love Bosnia, Sylvie said. Next week I'm going back.

Something then about teaching English there for the summer, but Timmy couldn't hear over the noise in his ears. *Leaving.* When Sylvie touched his arm, current flowed to his shoulder. Chairs were going up on the tables. I guess it's closing time, she said.

Timmy woke the next morning knowing he could wait for her. He prayed, awkwardly, *Thank you, Jesus, for your presence in my life.* Sometimes the idea of grace overwhelmed him, sometimes it made him suspicious. This time, both at once.

He saw Sylvie once more before she left, at AA where they couldn't talk much. While everyone shared, her face animated in the way of people more interested in others than in themselves. Timmy memorized her eyes, her mouth, the hollow at the base of her throat. Afterwards in the parking lot, he chose trusting she'd be back over asking for the actual date. He had 125 days clean and sober.

He kept her with him at JobWorks and in his apartment on top of the ice cream store. Mostly chaste thoughts: he imagined sex with her, sure, but often what came to mind was sitting shoulder to shoulder at Faith during worship and going out afterwards to eat. He wanted to tell her about his mom, who still lived in the doublewide where they'd moved after Timmy's dad left. She'd more or less quit parenting when he and Leah hit their teens, and she drank, but Timmy loved her. He wanted to tell Sylvie the idea for the bakery had come one day when he'd gone over and his mom's place was clean and she'd made bread, and the smell said they'd both be okay.

By now it was full-on spring—green everywhere and breezy-warm during the day. Usually spring was a season that belonged to other people, but this year was different. Timmy set out chairs on his deck; he picked up his bass and began practicing. He went to meetings, daily when he was lonely or too much in his head.

The feeling for Sylvie stayed. It had been a while since Timmy was interested in a woman when he wasn't high. When he was using, it was sex. Sober, it was more complicated. Sober, he could be intense.

His whole life, his expectations of others had followed him like a dog. Disappointment, too. Which was why he'd started using in the first place.

But that spring the dog was good, and calm, not desperate. One Tuesday after P&W Timmy went down front and asked if they could use anyone else on guitar. So that was Sunday afternoons, learning the bass lines to *I Surrender* and *El Shaddai* and a couple dozen other songs. The first time he played live with the band at a Tuesday service, it felt right. He thought about Sylvie coming home from Bosnia and them being onstage together.

He still couldn't tell the gospel of Luke from those of Matthew and Mark, and Jesus-is-the-only-way passages gave him trouble. But Pastor Mac's sermons about renewal sounded different knowing he was Sylvie's father. And the music. Jesus had always been a symbol, but now he felt real. Timmy understood why Faith was packed on Sundays. With the mill all but gone, the town hollowed out, it made people feel things could get better again.

You think too much, the P&W drummer told him when Timmy talked about this. Timmy laughed—he did. It's simple, the drummer said. We're sinners, we have to step away from pride. The drummer's name was Rick. Timmy liked him, so he went along. But he thought: it wasn't sin as much as it was people in Redham had forgotten who they were. Which meant they didn't know how to live or what to teach their kids. If you asked Timmy, it came down to the mill calling the shots all those years, giving people enough to keep them quiet and working hard, then cutting jobs when profits dropped. Redham was hurting. People were at Faith looking to fill themselves back up.

Including him. His dad had waited years to get rehired after the mill laid him off. Timmy had waited with him. Family dinners out and trips to the beach ended. His dad grew mean. Then he left. His mom signed up for MaineAid, but it wasn't enough. She started shopping the Dollar Store for real. Mac and cheese for a quarter. Liter of Sprite, ninety-nine cents. Eventually she found a job waitressing the Denny's late shift. Timmy and Leah carried each other the best they could, which wasn't very well. Timmy skipped school. Leah stopped eating for a while. He was using by fifteen, out of school and on probation by seventeen. Probation— he'd driven too high one night. Then he screwed that up and got sent to jail.

If you were lucky and lived long enough, you eventually realized you had to get to know your need and carry it with you. Take charge. The first time Timmy got sober, he'd been pissed whenever he heard a high-end engine below his apartment. It meant Bix or another dealer was trolling downtown. Timmy wanted them gone. But take out Bix and the rest, and others would move in. Or people would cook for themselves. In the end, you had to want to give it up, bad, and commit. You could still get overtaken— Timmy had, three times. Now whenever he heard Bix, he prayed for the need to be gone in Redham and in him.

Mid-July: AA almost every day, JobWorks, Faith on Sundays and Tuesday nights. Redham was at its best in summer. Trees in the park leafed out, flowers at the edges of lots, filling the broken pavement. Once in a while Rick came over. He was sober, too, so it worked. Timmy mixed Nestea and served chips with dip, then they jammed out on the porch. Rick could pick up songs and sing them, which meant Timmy sometimes got to sit and listen. At least until dusk, when the mosquitos drove them inside. Rick played P&W, and also pop. Weird how much they were alike. Take the lyrics to '*Iris*'. Listening to Rick sing them, Timmy thought about Sylvie, and he thought about Jesus, and wanting them to know who he, Timmy, was.

One afternoon while Rick was playing, Timmy got a text. It was from her. *Hi Timothy. Hoping you are well and enjoying summer.*

He sucked down the rest of his Nestea to steady himself. Timothy—that part made him smile. Formal. Biblical. He wrote, *I'm good, thanks for your note Sylvie. Hope you're doing well too.* Thought about it, added, *You are special,* and sent it. Nothing back. Maybe he'd said too much. Or not enough. Most of what he wanted to say would sound weird in a text anyway. Still, she'd reached out.

The first mosquito landed on his arm. Timmy let it bite, watched its belly swell and allowed it to fly unsteadily away.

What he'd like to tell Sylvie was that he thought about her a lot and couldn't wait to see her. That after he graduated JobWorks in December, he'd start saving for the bakery. He wondered whether she'd found AA in Bosnia. She'd said her father thought mission work was good because it was outer-focused. Timmy had seen how she listened, though, eyebrows steepled in concern. It wasn't self-absorption that made her drink. But—maybe Sylvie didn't need a meeting. Maybe she had enough else to see her through. Everyone in AA knew some had it easier than others. She might be one of them—some folks were built to make it, others not so much. In his family, Timmy and his mom had it tough, Leah less so. She'd been using off and on for years and getting by.

That night after Rick left, Timmy got to thinking about what he had to offer Sylvie. After JobWorks, Timmy would likely wind up doing appliance repair in Redham. No union wages there. It would take years to get the bakery. And his sobriety—knowing addiction was an illness didn't make it easier to stay clean.

He called Leah at work at the Ramada. She said, Timmy, just see what happens when she gets back.

Leah was practical and tough. A few weeks earlier they'd met up at Friendly's for dinner, then headed to Walmart to buy Trey sneakers. Inside the store, he'd begged for a Lego. Leah told him no, told him to stop. Trey didn't. So she packed him into the car and drove home. No shoes that night. Timmy couldn't have done it, but he bet Trey wouldn't whine the next time they went to Walmart.

September came, a few leaves on the ground in the mornings. Then one Sunday Sylvie was there at the evening service, sitting up front.

Timmy recognized her hair, even longer than it had been four months earlier. Down to her waist now. Excitement ran through him—*finally*. He considered moving up to be with her, but the service was beginning and anyway he needed time to gather himself. He stood up to sing, sat to pray. His heart drummed. He said, Thank you, Jesus, unselfconsciously for once. *Sylvie was back.*

He'd only come tonight because he'd played the morning service, which meant he'd mostly missed the sermon. Pastor Mac walked on stage, even more worked up than usual. I'm here to celebrate our Lord tonight, he said. I think you are too. Cheers and clapping, a few foot stomps. Amen. That's right. Pastor Mac got everyone up and shaking hands. Timmy stood, eyes on Sylvie, but she didn't turn around.

She was with a brown-haired man Timmy took to be her brother—Rick had said she had two—and a woman Timmy thought he recognized from the church office. Pastor Mac started talking about resurrection and related words that began with r. *ReAppear, ReVivify, ReSurge* came up in bullets on the screen up front.

We must pursue these as Christ-followers, Pastor Mac said, but Timmy couldn't concentrate. What should he say first to Sylvie?

He heard Leah as if she were with him in the pew: Focus on *her*—and of course that's what he'd do, ask about Bosnia, her teaching, what it was like there. Everything else would wait.

Afterwards he went down front. People were hugging her—Timmy realized how much Faith was Sylvie's. Finally, she noticed him. She smiled. Her tan filled in the freckles on her face.

Sylvie, he said. It's great to see you. He got the words out easily.

Stood square, held himself back from embracing her himself.

A look of caring on her face—but that was all. Things started to go cottony in Timmy's head. Sylvie leaned in. How are you?

Fine, he lied.

This is Amar, she said. And his sister Rana.

Amar put a hand on Sylvie's arm. Timmy wanted to knock it away. His throat clenched. She was being polite. Four and a half months, and it came down to this? He'd gotten it wrong. No. He knew she knew him.

Sylvie said she was home for two weeks. *They* were home, she said.

Timmy left the sanctuary. He had 230 days sober. He hadn't told his sponsor about Sylvie, and now he wouldn't. Didn't want to talk to Rick, either. He went home and lit his candles, and when that and toast did nothing he got back in his truck and drove over to the Ramada. One look at him, Leah knew. She shook her head, poured them coffee. It won't feel so terrible in the morning, she told him, but they both knew it would. Trey will be with me but I'll call you, Leah said.

Now the dog that followed him was sullen and reproachful— *it knew this would happen.* Back at the apartment, Timmy's rooms smelled like sour milk from the ice cream downstairs. He opened windows, let the cold air in. Got through the night. Morning, the Harvest Parade came down Broad Street, and people were in and out of the shop for cones. Timmy stayed upstairs, the buoyancy more than he could take. Disappointment was turning into anger—at himself, his parents, Redham. Not Sylvie.

By mid-afternoon the street was empty. Around 3:00 he heard dual exhaust. Bix down below in his Supra, looking for unmet needs. Timmy felt his own. His mouth and his eyes watered. He wanted. One time. Wanted. It was never that far away.

Did Bix look up, or did Timmy open the window first? Bix slowed and parked. Timmy sat on the couch. Surrender settled over him.

The dog was bitter. Timmy thought about how he and his mom and Leah never really got it together after his dad left—their dismal little Christmases and birthdays, Thanksgivings with turkey breasts because the whole bird was too hard, and how much he intended to be a different kind of man from his father. Be someone who stayed. But Sylvie couldn't take the chance, the chances. Timmy understood. How could she? How could anyone?

Bix knocked on the door. Timmy didn't move. It's open, he

said.

Leah stood there. Timmy stared—You have Trey today.
Don't worry about that, Leah said. Get up, we're going for a ride.
Timmy looked out the window. No sign of the Supra. In his mind he had already used. *She's taking me to rehab.* The familiar shame. He didn't look at her face. In the car he sat silently, only figured out they were on their way to the beach when Leah left the highway and headed down the peninsula.

About ten miles in, the road rose up, and the ocean spread before them. It had been Timmy's favorite view since he was a kid. He glanced at Leah. The beach wouldn't do much for him today. But— thanks, he said, it's beautiful. She nodded. This is what they did for each other, stepped up when they could. Out of his apartment, Timmy was relieved it was Leah who'd knocked, not Bix. He didn't want to go to sleep nights with a rocks-loaded pipe beside him for the morning. And he did not want rehab, the reminders everywhere that he hadn't made it, and the tedium.

Leah parked in the lot at Beach Eats. Timmy got out, put his hands on the hood and leaned over. He felt weak. The day was clear-skied and warm.

Leah touched his back. Let's have some clams, she said. My treat.

It was easy to get service this late in the season. They sat out on the deck, with a table of teens and a couple with a baby nearby. The smells of sunscreen and beer made Timmy lonelier. The clams came, fried and steamers. They ate quietly. Timmy waited for Leah to tell him he'd been foolish.
Let's go for a walk, she said when they finished.

The surf was down, tide on its way out. The sand was right for walking. Signs of Sylvie everywhere—the serious blue of the ocean her eyes; the inner shine of shells her skin.
Leah picked up the pace. Chilly, she said.

Timmy wasn't. He took off his shoes, rolled up his jeans and veered toward the water. Very cold. It was never warm, now it was on its way back to frigid. In another ten minutes they reached the open stretch of beach at the state park. Darker now, as if the ocean was suck-ing away the light along with the water. Timmy's feet had gone numb, and he liked that.

Three days from now, he would show up at Leah's with pizza to thank her for today. Rick would be waiting when he drove home, and they'd sit out on the porch and play. Timmy would stay away from

Faith, but mornings and nights he'd pray, and the Spirit would still be there. December would come, graduation, and he'd find a job at Comeau's Appliance. The Sunday before Christmas he would bring a tree over to his mom's. He'd have 310 days clean and sober.

Want to run, Leah asked. I'm freezing.
Timmy did. The sand was hard underfoot. His feet thawed and ached. The ocean was vast, indifferent, and he liked that too. Leah's arms pumped. Her hair flew back. Timmy got carried along, and the dog was quiet.

It was nearly dark by the time they reached the car. A gull watched from a nearby piling as Timmy sat in the sand to brush off his feet and put on shoes. The tide was on its way back up. Waves crested and drained but kept gaining ground. Once when he was a kid he'd stayed in the guest house attached to Beach Eats. One big room, his parents in the double bed and him and Leah in bunks. Kitchenette in the corner. What was he, eleven?
Leah started the car and the gull flapped off. Timmy stood. That time in the guest house he'd woken the next morning to the smell of pancakes and sausage, his dad making a breakfast Timmy still remembered.

*- CB Andreson*

# Riding home in your White Valiant after the Opera

(a Duplex – after Jericho Brown)

I remember that ride back from the city,
when we stopped to swing around light poles in the parking lot,

     light pooled in the parking lot.
     I couldn't believe that love budded in us.

I couldn't believe that love fell into us
green and gentle and brilliant as glass.

     We were green and gentle and resilient as grass.
     The moon – descending out of itself.

The moon – was there a moon?
I can't remember, only that stars sprinkled us with sugar.

     I can only remember sugar and stars,
     and were there streetlights?  Did we kiss in the parking lot?

Was there a moon?  Or streetlights? I can't remember kissing,
only dancing, light poles, and that ride back home from the city.

*- Elizabeth Vrenios*

# A Medicinal Catalogue

One stole from me my body with every breath,
one with garlanded noose tempted death.

One collapsed beneath the moonless night,
one upon my shins colored twilight.

One tortured my days grasped in fists,
one, in terror, slumber kissed.

One crowned me in futile bandages,
one further dissolved the adages.

One speckled my face in mourning,
one a frivolous pearl adorning.

One foretold a futile plea,
one scattered about the shards of me.

One revealed to the mouths of tombs,
one, for a moment, my heartbeat resumes.

One starved me of the love I knew,
one lamented my sanity through.

*- Kaitlin Kan*

# In November

the horses return,
    night-watchers, gentle grazers,

holy presences
    of winter fur and eyes
        of dark water's light.

They return
    to share comfort and joy –
        the comfort of animal husbandry,

the tender care
    of daily watering,
        feeding, cleaning, brushing,

bedding-down,
    sheltering,
        veterinary hands,

and the joy of return,
    the white mare rolling,
        rolling her Dionysian downhill roll.

Neither north winds
    nor cold rains chill
        the steady flow of warmth,

the fire in their breaths.
    Noses nuzzle and kiss
        hearth and home,

kiss their feast
    moveable as flying feet
        kiss the old Holly Farm,

making sacred
    their pasture,
        their table spread

beneath conifers
    in the wilderness
        of their hearts.

*- M. Ann Reed*

# BLUE CLOAK EMROIDERED
# WITH SWALLOWS

Each pantomime is rewarded with mistakes, the ocean with the mission church burned down.  Let one thousand books disappear and the host reward you.  The resin survives the birth of reason.  It is the conviction of actuality where the desire for union is prolonged and made beautiful.  The holy is disappointing.  Invent something during the childhood of duration. The flaw removed from the diamond, the head bowed in grief, dark centuries in the heart of arrogance, contradictions as churchyard crusades where calibrated dimensions are allowed because they believe the cleared text is the forgiven word.  History involves river crossings and neglected mountains.  The value of a rainbow in the desert is a healing cry abandoned by map makers.  It is true that solemn faces once roamed the earth with dry flowers, broken bracelets, and the first egg yolk eaten by the wise.  The Bible?  No, only fingers in the sand.

*- Ray Gonzalez*

# SNAP

Let other people speak for you.
Their foreheads are as sweaty as yours.
Close the white door because
the world is about to snap.
Let the dictator smell your feet.
You have been running for 68 years
and your heels are sore.
When the dictator snorts,
the pandemic will arrive
and he will snap.

Let others pray for you.
Their faith is not lost
in the dusty desert wind.
Their practice of genuflection
makes their knees snap
on the benches of sin.
When they ask you for favors,
do not make a sound.
Time is present in the dust
inside the candle holders where
someone found the ashes
of your notes.

Let others speak because
silence comes from a mother's
hands after she snapped at
you because she insisted men
were digging a tunnel under
her house.
It is not the way to get home
because the unadorned Mexican
trees prefer the fighting rooster

with its bleeding claws, razors
strapped to its legs so it can
slash to the center of the light
where there is a revolution no
one acts on, buckets of blood
cleansing the color of the roses
raining down in the church yard.

*- Ray Gonzalez*

# Le Mot Juste

Sometimes, I wish I was brave
as these crocus buds not yet waving,
for whom silence is eternity
and everything began yesterday;

instead, I cling to a stubborn faith
in an ancient language
which still can't convey
the religiousness of plain light.

But then, I don't know, I want to say,
somehow, maybe—
a decision you can't make
is one that's already been decided—

like the way the fragile skies
and ladies in gray keep weeping
and weeping each spring, but Jesus
keeps getting crucified anyway.

*- Dan Smart*

# SILENCE SPEAKS

Listen:
just underneath
the clamor

of the Earth
as she's heaving

her second-
to-last breath;

just in-between
our having come this far
reluctantly

and the chaotic way
we are cleft
as we leave—

an absence
interposes;

a silence
that speaks.

There are moments, it says,
when we can't act
as we must;

there are endings
far more everlasting
than heaven—

yet less abrupt
than death.

*- Dan Smart*

# Angular grace is modulated

in the sky's wilderness where a blind comet dreams of God
resting in a hammock vacationing between twinned worlds.

Memory softens and then is reshaped in amber;
inside turns out & then collapses. Another dream

becomes a single wave where heart & eye devour each other.
Blisters celebrate the annunciation. Tomorrow burns

bright & savory. Kindness arrays itself cunningly
in elegant sorrow. Wobbles and shakes its jowls.

*- Richard Weaver*

# BY THE BANKS OF THE CHESAPEAKE AND OHIO

Where we crouched
by the canal, our lanky
tongues knotted
with salt, with slats
of whiplash.

There we splashed
the hash of our fire,
reefing without caution
or fear in the bushy banks.

We were the rub
of lip and root,
plinking our troth
into slurp and pearl.

Nothing could rot us
back then, young
and indignant and giddy
with the insurgency
of long trammeled surges
that broke out even
under the roof
of the moon-driven wind.

*- Tom Daley*

# IDEAS

--for Diane Wakoski

Not an ounce of poetry in me tonight.

Probably no prose either.
Art is a lobster shell.

*

My mouth tastes like metal
due to vitamin D3 pills.

I'm supposed to have more energy
when I get my vitamin D up.

Like insomnia?

*

In a poetry workshop Diane Wakoski said,
"Most people never have an idea."

That "idea" is an over-used word.
She said, "Thomas Edison had ideas."

Statements such as that
made it very difficult to write poetry.

*

"Why is that a play?" someone asked
Frank O'Hara.

I don't remember his quote, but the paraphrase is:
"It's a play because you call it a play."

*

The rain has lightened-up.

When I first moved to California

I kept thinking, What the fuck's up
with the roofs.

They looked so shittily made.
So flimsy.

Then I realized they don't have to hold snow.
So you hear the rain much more in California

than in Michigan if you're inside a house.
I suppose that means we are "closer to nature"

in California.
And I also wondered

what the fuck was up with all the conservatives in California,
I thought I was moving to a liberal haven.

Many of my dumb-ass neighbors keep voting down gay rights,
and they vote down legalizing pot,

even one of my acquaintances, who's the lead singer in a rock band,
and likes to drink, voted against legalizing pot.

But still I love California, and have now lived here 25 years.
I also love Michigan.

And Little Falls, New York.
I am not a big fan of Rochester, New York.

I don't think you could give me enough money to live in Rochester, New York.
Although every man has his price.


*


After reading 3975 pages of Proust
I wrote a story.

I think it's a fine story.

Davin thinks it should be called, "Brokeback Mountain: The Clover Pool
Years."

Davin is quite the kidder.
I'm calling it "Story 1."

He is not amused.

*



The older I get—I'm 50 now—
the less I want to be around people.

I see the benefit Proust got locking himself away
the last 15 years of his life.

Partially that was not by choice—it was because of asthma
before there were good drugs for asthma.

But even with the good drugs
people still die of asthma.

*


I forgot to take my mouthful of chemo
yesterday but no problem, I just made up for it.

I have the heat on.

A colleague at "work" told me today
it will snow in Pasadena.

I had 25 years of winter in Rochester, New York
and in Drayton Plains, Michigan.

Really, I do not think it will be snowing in Pasadena any time soon.

It's 50 degrees right now in Pasadena
at 12:39 a.m.

and some of the locals think this might lead to snow.
And we can't really

blame this on the public schools.
I do think they taught repeatedly about the freezing temperature of water.

There are simple parts of life
that leave me confused every day too.

I'm not saying I'm above it.
But—I guess I'm an elitist and a snob—

I would just suspect there would be a little basic knowledge
about states of matter, the First Amendment.


But so many Americans today
don't understand that equality and freedom are for everyone.

*


It has been raining steady for 10 hours.
The snow pack in the Sierras was 195% of normal before this storm.

So we will have no drought this summer.
Well, no drought concerning water.

We do seem to have some drought of common sense,
basic knowledge and equality.

*


This poem
is an example of how to turn

a really shitty idea
into great art.

- Craig Cotter

**THE BIG C-130 HERCULES THUNDERED DOWN** down through the clouds, its broad, silver wings glistening in the African sunlight. The four Allison engines roared as the plane found its altitude, pulled up and leveled. Ahead, through the narrow cockpit window, Jake Henley could see the mountain pass, a distinct V-shaped notch in the ridge.

"Is that it?" he shouted back.

Kamifu, his Tanzanian aide, leaned in over his shoulder and looked out the narrow cockpit window. "Yes, Mr. Jake. That is it."

"How far from there?"

"Three *dakikas*."

"Minutes, Kamifu. How many minutes?"

"Not many minutes, Mr. Jake."

Jake looked back at Kamifu's black face but could only see his white eyes flashing and the scraggly white hairs on his chin.

"About how many?" Jake asked.

"About ten. You stay low. Must get very low, or they shoot us out of the sky. Boom! *Wafu*—we dead."

"Well, we don't want that."

They had left Nairobi four hours earlier, at the crack of dawn, and now the sun was high and bright and shone sharply off the silvery nose of the plane. The glare caused Jake to squint, even from behind the shield of his sunglasses. Kamifu, however, seemed unaffected by the bright rays. A lifetime beneath the Savannah's hot sun had hardened his pupils and produced a natural ultraviolet filter. Jake glanced out the side window at the landscape streaming by below. There were groves of acacia trees and a river and some small lakes. The land rose sharply beneath them, sloping up toward the mountain pass ahead.

"You stay low," Kamifu said again.

When Jake pushed the wheel forward, the plane dipped, and Kamifu lurched forward, clinging to the back of Jake's seat to keep his balance. The engines roared again, and the plane lifted slightly, rising with the earth. The altimeter faithfully held at one hundred and fifty feet.

"That was good, Mr. Jake," Kamifu said, showing his broad, white-toothed smile.

"It wasn't intentional, Kamifu."

"What?"

"Never mind."

"I go now. Get ready for drop."

"How will I know? How will I know where to find the mark?"

"You will know, Mr. Jake. There will be a space, wide as the Savannah itself. No problem. Trust me."

Jake Henley frowned.

"I get ready, okay?"

"Yeah, you do that."

Kamifu's tall shadow disappeared into the darkness of the cargo hull while Jake locked both hands onto the steering wheel and fixed his eyes out the cockpit window. He felt flushed now, hot even. He pulled open the side window and let the air rush in, and as he did, it blew his hair in wild little swirls. He could feel his heart pounding, pumping like a speedy metronome. He glanced up at a photograph of a young woman paper-clipped to a wire above the cockpit window. She stood next to an acacia tree with two Maasai children by her side. Now, ahead, was only blue sky, as he was approaching the top of the ridge. The vintage plane rattled all about him, the engines hummed smoothly on either side. With slow, skillful movements, he pointed the nose of the plane up through the gap in the ridge.

Back in the cargo hold, Kamifu cranked the bomb-bay door open. His lean, wiry frame leaned into it, pulling down hard on the crank-lever. The rear doors slowly widened, and as they did, the sound of wind rushing into the hold increased in volume and ferocity, as did the sound of the Allison engines. He was dressed in shorts and a green army tunic, and the wind whipped the cloth against his thighs and his arms. With one last long crank he locked the bomb-bay door lever in place. Then he staggered to the edge of the opened ramp and looked down.

The good African earth rushed by beneath him—rugged terrain speckled with green acacia trees and the gnarled tops of baobab, rising to boulder-strewn slopes and rocky cliffs. Above, stacked on freight pallets were the cargo bins, queued-up on huge roller coaster rails that led out the rear ramp. He walked back to the first bin and patted its plywood side.

"You go down to my people, now," he said. Then in Swahili, "*Tufanye sote bidii.* With hearts strong and true. You make them well."

His eyes were laughing, and a soft smile came to his face. He took a place near the drop lever, stood and waited. Through the gaping rear doors he could see the mountainside rapidly ascending.

***

On the ground, just beyond the notch in the mountains, dug in trenches beneath large camouflaged netting, were several members of the Hutu militia, *Interhamwe.* All former regulars of the Rwandese Army, they fought now against the new government and the *Forces Armees Rwandaises.* They had taken part in the great genocide, the bloodbath of Africans killing Africans which had split the country in civil war. On their hands was the blood of thousands of Tootsies, hacked with machetes or shot with the same guns they held now against a lone steel beast coming rapidly their way.

High on a mound of earth stood their young Lieutenant, Kayomba. Like the others, he still wore the war-torn uniform of the old regime. He held a pair of binoculars in one hand and pointed skyward with a handgun in the other.

"*Sikisa! Hapo!* Over there!"

They could all hear the plane's engines coming, and with his direction the soldiers turned and focused and pointed their rifles just above the southern outcropping rocks. They had one vintage Browning fifty-caliber machinegun, which swiveled on its tripod in the direction of the approaching sound.

"*Ngojea angu amrisha!*" Lieutenant Kayomba yelled. "Wait for my command."

His large black hand held his handgun high.

The droning of the turboprop engines grew louder, and out of nowhere, flying barely above the ridge, the belly of the C-130 emerged bright and large.

"*Sasa!*" Lieutenant Kayomba pulled the trigger on his handgun, repeatedly, following the belly of the plane. Likewise his men fired, and the pedestal-mounted machine gun, all in unison, tracked the plane as it streaked across the Rwandan sky. The sound of their guns spattered and popped like a long string of firecrackers.

But the plane had come in so low and fast it was gone before they knew it. Mostly they were firing at the tail as it trailed away. Lieutenant Kayomba dropped an empty clip, slapped in another, and fired a few more rounds. Then he lowered his handgun and watched as the plane sped away and dropped into the valley beyond.

"*Chafu taka ngurauwe!*" he hollered. "Filthy pigs!"

He looked down at the young soldier behind the machinegun. Incompetence leads to defeat, he thought, as though cursing himself. He walked down to the soldier and whacked him in the back of the head with his opened hand.

***

Inside the plane, the rapid pinging sounds of hundreds of rounds whacking through the metal frame and ricocheting all over had caused Jake to duck down. He listened until the pings diminished, and when they had ceased, he called back into the cargo bay, "Kamifu! We made it."

Ahead of him, the savannah opened like a huge curtain, filling the one-hundred-and-eighty degree view of the cockpit. And below him now, approaching rapidly and moving on the ground like a giant wave, rippling as if made of velvet, was a vast, colorful sea of humanity. Thousands of refugees had gathered in this valley between the mountains. They had made the week-long journey out of Rwanda to the northern border of Tanzania to evade genocide and starvation.

Looks like a million ants, Jake thought. It is a million ants.
And there in the center of it all, as Kamifu promised, was a long wide lane, cleared by the ground crew for the drop. He'd have to get low, real low, or the bins would crush the crowd.

Jake pushed forward on the wheel, then pulled up and leveled at an altitude of barely five hundred feet. As he came thundering over the heads of thousands of refugees he looked out the side window, and could see the people clearly now, the garments of reds and yellows and blues. There in the middle was a tall, thin African woman standing above the crowd, her arms stretched skyward, holding a baby up toward the plane. As he flew over he turned his head and his eyes followed her aft as she pivoted the baby in his direction. He looked forward. The drop zone was just before them.

Jake took hold of the intercom transceiver and called back to Kamifu.

"Get ready, buddy. We're coming up on it. I'll give you the mark."

Slowly, steadily, holding the transceiver in his right hand, he leveled the wings and lined up the nose in the center of the long clearing. The ground, rushing by in a blurry mix of colorful garments, suddenly parted as though by the will of Moses. Then there was nothing but barren earth with the shadow of the plane skirting over it.

"Now. Now, Kamifu. Let 'em go."

Jake held the plane as steady as he could, trying to give Kamifu as clean and clear a lane as possible. He anticipated the cargo-bumping a pilot would normally feel dropping cargo aft, but it never came. He tried to look back from the side window, but the swell of the plane's body obstructed his view. He placed the transceiver back in its bracket, widened the window, removed his sunglasses, and stuck his head all the way out, so far that the wind flattened the hair on the back of his head. Now, the angle providing sufficient vision to the rear, he could see the tail of the plane and the long clearing trailing aft, but there were no cargo bins falling to the ground.

What the Hell?
He grabbed the microphone and repeated the command. "Now, Kamifu. Now."

He stuck his head back out the window, looking and waiting, but he saw nothing. In front of him the clearing was coming to an end, and beyond an outcropping of rocks rose abruptly from the savannah.

"Kamifu, can you hear me?" He thumped the transceiver against the console. "Can you hear me?"

The rise in the earth was coming up quickly. "Hold up, Kamifu. I'll come back around." He slapped the microphone back in its bracket.

The massive river of refugees below suddenly swallowed up the clearing. He pulled back on the wheel, and as the engines roared and the nose of the cargo-heavy plane rose steeply above the outcropping of rocks, he saw a flash of light. Then a second flash, and he knew he had been fired upon. Coming from the outcropping at a tremendous speed were two fireballs, each trailing long curly tails of smoke. They came directly at him. He cranked the wheel hard left. All four engines screamed. The frame of the aging plane chattered and creaked, and both missiles skimmed past on his starboard side and headed toward the sun.

Jake trembled now. Sweat poured down his face and neck. His mouth was parched. "I should have taken that job flying for UPS," he mumbled.

After swinging wide westward, he was back on the transceiver to Kamifu. Again, there was no response. Jake stared at the transceiver, and then tossed it down.

He had gained enough altitude now to clear the rugged mountains west. He leveled the wings, heading straight for Zaire, and put on the autopilot. Then he scrambled aft down the cluttered connecting corridor, climbing over cables and boxes.

The cargo hold howled with wind. Immediately he saw that the floor was riddled with tiny holes, and bright pencil-thin columns of light shone up through them. Across the bay Kamifu lay flat near the drop lever, blood streaming from his long body. It sprayed about the floor and walls, whipped by the wind.

Jake staggered forward, having to brace himself against the hull. He dropped to Kamifu's side and shook him. Kamifu's cotton shirt flapped wildly in the updraft, but he did not move.

"Hold on," Jake cried above the droning of the engines. But it was useless, he knew. He was gone.

Jake made his way back to the cockpit through the corridor, breathing heavily. By the time he was back in the pilot seat, he was ready to kill. He screamed and slammed his palm against the steering wheel.

"Those dirty bastards. Those dirty, dirty bastards."

The plane had gone far beyond the pilgrimage now. Rushing below was onlY the dry earth and the wide shadow of the plane's body and wings. He released the autopilot and turned the wheel so that the plane made a long, arching curve southwest.

He was alone now, without the aid of his trusty friend. And there was no one on the ground who could help him. He considered abandoning the mission and heading back to Nairobi. He was not a soldier. He was only a volunteer in a faraway land. He looked at the photograph paper-clipped to the wire above the cockpit window. The youthful female face stared back at him.

"Okay, Jake Henley," he muttered. "You're going to do this."

He continued his curve, eventually going from southwest to due south. In the time it took to turn the plane around, he had traveled a considerable distance from the large savannah where the refugees had gathered, and from the mountain pass where Lieutenant Kayomba and his men waited with their guns. It gave him time to consider how best to do this. He could not approach from the east or west, he knew, for the clearing ran north and south, narrowly between the waves of refugees. He could not make the drop in the foothills east or west, because it might fall into the hands of the Interhamwe, or it could cause a stampede of some kind whereby, without the guidance of the ground crew, hundreds could be crushed and killed. Coming from the north he would have to contend with the steep outcropping of rocks and the surface-to-air missiles again, and there'd be miles of open-air exposure before and after arriving at the drop-zone, giving the assailants plenty of time to see him coming and take aim. No, from the south was the only way, over Lieutenant Kayomba and his band of soldiers with small arms fire. They would never expect him, Jake thought. No one would be so crazy to fly over that again. And flying low as he did before, he knew their firing window would be short and quick and more focused on the tail, not the engines.

He looked at the fuel gauge. It was down to a quarter.

"Besides, there's not enough fuel to go all the way back north and get back to Nairobi," he said.

He straightened the plane toward the range of brown mountains from which he had flown in from Kenyatta Airport. When he was far enough south, beyond earshot of the soldiers waiting in the V-shaped pass, he turned the plane north again. He thought of Kamifu: smiling one minute, and then lying dead in the cargo hold the next. He saw the African woman on the ground, holding her baby high toward the plane. And he looked at the photograph of the young woman again, as though to give him strength.

***

Lieutenant Kayomba stood on a mound of earth in the narrow hollow of the ridge. He had watched the plane, a silver speck on the horizon, narrowly evade the surface-to-air missiles. And he had followed it west until it disappeared beyond the skyline of mountains. At first he thought it was heading to Kinshasa or perhaps on a long, looping route to Nairobi over the Great Rift Valley and Lake Victoria. So he was surprised to hear the distant droning of the engines. He brought the binoculars to his face and scanned the horizon, and he saw the plane, several kilometers off, popping in and out of view beyond the western mountains. He watched it head further south until it was finally gone behind the ridge. Then he raised his hand for his soldiers to see him, pointed in the direction of the plane, and shouted, "*Andaliwa.* Be ready."

He scurried down to the young soldier behind the Browning machinegun and shoved him aside. He took hold of the trigger-grips.

The sound of the engines drew steadily closer. They could hear the plane approaching, but could not see it. All the soldiers stood poised and ready; their weapons pointed in the direction where they knew it would come.

***

Jake was trembling now, remembering Kamifu's words: "Keep it low, keep very low." He reached up and touched the photo of the young woman, and he said, "Be with me now, Baby."

Through the windshield, the mountain pass approached at a phenomenal pace, something akin to the streaking terrain in the viewfinder of a Star Wars video game. He had decided not to make it easy for them. He'd come in from a slightly different angle, and drop even lower. He throttled up as the mountain walls approached on either side. The aged, metal frame rattled and creaked from the tremendous torque of the lift. The plane followed the contour of the earth as would a skillful bird. Coming up in the cockpit windows was the low notch in the mountains. Then, holding the steering wheel straight out before him, both hands fisted, he let out a loud, involuntary cry.

The bottom of the plane flashed white over Lieutenant Kayomba and his men. As soon as it appeared they let loose hundreds of rounds, pounding the steel belly and fuselage and the wing undercarriage. Their guns followed the plane the best they could, but it was nearly impossible. They basically had to swing their rifles from south to north in one fast, fluid motion.

From the plane's cockpit, the fire spitting from the soldiers' gun barrels looked like the flashing bulbs of a hundred press cameras. Jake cringed at the sound of all the bullets ripping through the metal. It was all about him now. The pinging seemed to sustain even longer than before. But like before, it was concentrated more toward the tail-end. One of the right engines sputtered, tossed some smoke, but kept going. Thirty seconds, and then a minute passed, and the pinging subsided. And then, one last ping against the rear fuselage and he heard no more. He pushed the wheel further forward and followed down the contour of the earth, sometimes only a matter of feet above pinnacles of rocks and craggy outcrops. Then, with the vast savannah spreading out before him, he leveled the plane and got some air between him and the earth.

Now coming up rapidly in the windshield was the huge exodus of refugees, and he could see the long, beautiful clearing opened by the ground crew. He dropped in low again, held steady, and lined up the wings. He watched the altimeter until it was perfectly level. Then he clicked on the autopilot and leaped to the rear.

The plane bounced turbulently as Jake scrambled through the connecting corridor. He stepped carefully over Kamifu's body, glancing down briefly at his lifeless face, to the edge of the bomb-bay where the drop lever was located. The wind rushing up from the opening took his hair straight back. Beneath him, flashing by in the gaping cargo bay doors, he saw the thousands of colorful shawls and tunics, and the thousands of black heads all squeezed together. Then, just as suddenly, came ground, only ground, and no people.

He grabbed hold of the drop lever and yanked down on it.

The cargo bins began to come down the rails. The first one dropped out the rear ramp, snapped taut its static line, and pulled free. The parachute ballooned open, and the crate drifted down toward the earth.

"Yeah!"

Then came the next food bin, and the next, each staggered on their freight pallets, coming down the rollers, dropping out the rear doors, and snapping free of their static line. Jake watched for a minute as each beautiful white parachute blossomed open and drifted downward, one after another. Then he scurried back to the cockpit, climbed into his seat, and clicked off the auto pilot.

The view out the cockpit window was a relieving sight. The outcropping of rocks from which the missiles had been fired before was still a distance away. He had timed it well.

No need to rush, he told himself. Finish the drop. Then pull off east.

He glanced back, out the side window. Beneath the tail of the plane the big, beautiful white parachutes continued blossoming and drifting downward and hitting the ground. The last parachute opened, its cargo crate drifted to the ground. Jake watched, giving it time, seeing no more crates coming out. The last one plowed up a cloud of dust that rose and covered the activity on the ground. He cranked the throttle and turned the wheel hard right and back. The engines roared, lifting the C-130 swiftly eastward into the Rwandese sky. Then the plane flattened into a course due east.

Jake swung his neck around and looked back at the outcropping of rocks. He saw nothing coming from it.

"Yes," he shouted and pounded his fist on the wheel.

He could feel his body shaking, the adrenalin still pumping through his veins. He held the wheel straight, throttle all the way down, wanting to get as far away from the rocks as he could, as quickly as he could. When he reached a distance of several kilometers he began to think about it. It seemed the drop had gone well, but he was not sure. He wanted to make sure he had done it right. He wanted to see the fruits of his labor. He began turning the plane in a big half-circle, back toward the drop site. He could come in perpendicular, from east to west, at a safe distance from gunfire.

In a matter of minutes, the plane had turned completely around. Slowly unrolling before him was the massive congregation of refugees—legions of them, coming together as one.

Jake dropped the plane down low. Then even lower, skimming over the top of the crowd. He looked out his side window, the warm air rushing in against his face, and saw the people clearly, their colorful garments swarming the cargo bins, broken open now. The people shoveled out pails of golden grain and corn. He could see the project workers, one standing atop an opened crate beneath a white safari hat, a thousand hands reaching up to him. He could see all the people cramming together, all the colors becoming one. And there, coming up rapidly off the port nose of the plane, was the tall, thin woman, holding her baby high in her outstretched arms, triumphantly, toward the plane.

*- Frank Scozzari*

# Ben,

your eyes feel good like going upstairs
to grab a pen or when I see running horses
Arizona Burger King.

You sometimes touch me like old photographs
of family I can no longer bring myself to look at.

When I read someone's fortune,
I show them how we change each other,
in this mosaic, of musical
soil & twirl, the Hanged Man
says you're still holding
on to parts
someone else
has let go.

Ben,

It takes so long to drive through Texas,
all the loud grand clouds ablaze above the midlands.


I'm turning my body in music, lifting my hands
high in night air, and a box fan cools & whirs
like wheels somewhere in a distance
that doesn't exist.

Ben,

poetry always seems bigger than me,
our best is what we'll call Art, so for now the drywall
and its doorframe with your name's initials will have to do, but tonight not the
plywood
I would rather sleep, just humans under sheets.

The Texas night and the loss of our rights,
and still, the wind is in my hand, San Antonio.

Long is the highway, but all of the stars.


Interstate 10, Texas 2018


*- Wyatt Welch*

# To my Husband as I Near my 54th Birthday

How time goes like an owl on silent wings
So that I'm surprised to find I am not young.
Thirty years with you have passed like a wink.
You are the one who truly knows my tongue.

I've a glimpse of age, then my youth again.
Darkness falls over the mountain, eroded.
I make sure you and I have heard the wind,
What the canyon verse I produce has boded.

But the wind dies out as do old curses.
May these lines stand like the north mountain
As I am like the wolf cub that nurses
At the river's teat, at such a fountain

That we two shall not die but in my word-play
Shall be ever young, light, and stay that way.

*- Robin Scofield*

# SUPERPOWERS

*After a photograph in the* New York Times

Formed from a torn tablecloth, his checkered cape
floats free behind him, arms spread,
one foot suspended in air, ready to leap

from the kitchen shelf into his father's arms.
He has his balance. A five-year-old boy with
superpowers. A boy ready for flight.

The boy will take flight soon with his father.
They will not fly, they will walk, perhaps more
than a hundred shadeless days. They will leave

behind the tablecloth, the kitchen,
the brilliant hues of the quetzal bird
flying across a woven blanket. The father

has surveyed his coffee fields, once fertile,
leaves now consumed in brown fungus,
no sooner rotting than passing their poison

to the next plant, leaving the belly of the boy
almost as empty as the belly of the father.
I wish him superpowers

to fly safely across borders
he knows they are not welcomed to cross,
spurned by a superpower as unyielding as his land.

*- Joanne Durham*

# TUMBLING

Tumbling
Tumbling
Tumbling...

There are no sides to reach out to
There is no bottom to hit

The place we left
Is gone
The place we are headed to
Doesn't exist

Everything in between
Is thin
And can't manifest

She points at my heart
With a finger
That isn't, asks:
Does it hurt?

I try to tell her
It is all a Dream—
But I have no mouth


*- William Waters*

# Under the Hood

THE NURSE MEASURES MY BLOOD PRESSURE, carefully, as if it's sugar glass under my skin instead of bone, and tells me that the doctor will see me soon. She won't quite look at me. I was here last week for a routine physical, my first in five years. Since I get insurance with my new administrative assistant job, it seemed wise. But then a nurse called and said something showed up abnormal in my bloodwork, and the doctor wanted me back in to discuss. Urgent, was the word she'd used. Now, I wish I'd never made the initial appointment. I regret ever taking the job.

I refuse to wait on the exam table. Instead, I sit on the plastic chair to the side and tuck into my oversized sweatshirt. The peach color on the walls tries to mask the medical smell, offset the posters about stroke awareness and smokers' lungs. Today I have on makeup, loads of blush. I don't want to look pale. Probably now I look flushed.

In the hallway, the nurses chat. Not about patient care, but about beds. "Where'd you get your mattress again?" I overhear one of them ask. "Mattress Firm," another answers. "It's expensive but get the Tempur-Pedic. My dog loves it."

I wonder how they do it, switch on and off. I remember when my mother and I took Lily, my cocker spaniel, to her first vet appointment. This was back when Lily was a puppy, and I was in high school. I didn't want a car when I turned sixteen. Instead, I wanted a dog. "Go outside," my mother said on the morning of my birthday. "There's a bunch of deer—you have to see." There were always deer where we lived, but my mother seemed so jazzed, her whole body a smile, so I opened the door. In the grass crouched a puppy with a yellow ribbon tied around its neck.

A few days later, my mother and I drove Lily to the veterinarian's office. I'd never had a dog before, only heaps of barn cats that a mobile vet sometimes came by to spay. With a dog, my mom said all the shots were important. The vet tech placed Lily on the exam table and told me how soft her caramel-colored fur felt, how strong her heart pounded. I was tired, I'd been up all night with the puppy, taking her out and petting her when she seemed scared, maybe missing her mom. My parents had also gifted me an oval-shaped dog bed, but instead I'd pulled her up to sleep in my arms. The veterinarian then came in, and my mom stroked my back as I stroked Lily's. "She's perfect, isn't she?" my mother said. I wasn't sure if she meant me or the dog. Either way, the vet agreed.

Lily peed on me while I carried her back to the car. I was wiping us both off when my mom and I heard a howl. I assumed it was an animal, but then I saw a woman clinging to a skeletal Dalmatian that kept slipping when it tried to stand. A vet tech rushed out to help, the same one who had laughed with me and kissed Lily's damp nose.

"That'll be the hardest part," my mother said. "When you one day have to say goodbye."

We didn't know then that my mom had cancer. It would be several weeks until she fainted in the kitchen while teaching me how to make chicken parmesan. Lily responded by licking my mother's hands, covered in the raw chicken smell. I kicked her back, hard, even though she was just doing what dogs do.

When my parents sat me down to explain the diagnosis, I didn't understand, because my mother looked as vibrant as ever, in a burgundy wrap dress and her hair long and shining. I thought the doctors must be wrong and wished they'd never run tests, never looked under the hood, as my dad had called it. But the experts were right. She died within six months. Two years later, I went to college, renting an off-campus apartment instead of a dorm so I could have Lily, leaving my father alone. Soon after, he met a woman online. They now live in Arkansas, running a B&B near her family.

If something happens to me, I wonder who will take care of my dog. My mom couldn't eat during her final days, but she was at home, so my dad and I cooked chai with butter and vanilla and placed the pan under her hospice bed. The room smelled like a bakery as her wet breaths crackled and I whispered that it was okay to go. Lily's older now, on diabetes medication, deaf and half-blind, her coat coarse and gray. She no longer sleeps in my bed, it's too difficult on her joints to jump on and off, so instead she curls up on the doggie bed my parents gave me all those years ago. Already, I crave her body. Already, she's a little gone. I want to tell the nurse that one day this will happen to her. Her dog may like the Tempur-Pedic now, but it won't last, so she better get ready. But she knows this. She opens doors into rooms that encompass different worlds every day. They see everyone here, babies, the old and the sick, those with minor ailments. Me.

"Thanks for waiting," the doctor says, swooping in and lowering himself onto the rolling stool, a dap of sweat on his sun-spotted forehead. Despite his busy morning, he doesn't log into the computer to review notes, instead softly holds my gaze. Without instruction I head to the exam table. I guess I do want to know. He says he has some information for us to discuss, together, and I nod, wanting this over, but because his eyes don't leave mine, I think I can take it, whatever it is he has to say.

*- Shannon Perri*

# Animal Tracks in Snow

I take delight in looking out in the
morning on a smooth field of snow
through which a solitary coyote or

deer has passed, evidence that we
live with animals who normally
don't like to advertise their presence

preferring not to be seen but then
the snow comes and we get evidence
of animal traffic, ships passing in

the night, of which we are totally
unaware except the snow makes it
visible in retrospect. I could imagine

angel traffic, angels passing by, except
there is nothing that corresponds to
snow, no such metaphor giving

retrospect. We have to detect them
differently and we have to want to
believe and be able to spin theories

in god-of-the-gaps fashion. Here is
your explanation, an angel came to
visit Mary and told her of the miracle

of conception how a single sperm cell,
against all odds, penetrates the ovum
and gets a welcome bringing gifts to the

party. So there is dancing and untwisting
of recombinant molecules and in the end
the spirit pops in. And so Mary signed on.

I'll do it, she said, and Joseph, her fiancé,

descendent of David, was joyful when he
got word of Mary's willingness. That is

taken as evidence of angels passing,
good things happen, traces in the snow.

*- James Stemmle*

# Little Fellow

**I'VE BEEN BOTTLE FEEDING HIM** now for two days and two nights, trying to keep him alive. Born three days ago, for some reason, he and Sheba can't figure out the nursing part of it. Maybe he's inherited that skittishness of his father Arazim. Over the phone, all the vet told us is that this can happen with a foal, and when it does, it just makes him shake his head and feel sad. He agreed with my dad that we could try to bottle-feed him, which we've done a couple times with lambs and calves. I'm in charge of it, so it's up to me—and I suppose the Blessed Virgin, and St. Francis, and anyone else I can think of. Why doesn't this little colt want to eat? Babies always want to eat.

Sleeping out by the barn in the back of the flatbed Chevy, I've set the alarm to ring every few hours so I can heat up thinned, sweetened milk to feed to him like I've done over the years with Jo, Beth, Tom, and Annie, our most recent new babies over the years.

Soft and fluffy as a boney and spindly teddy bear, the little colt is the light brown of a milky hot chocolate. Four white stockings reach up his long legs from his little hooves. A beautiful white blaze runs down the center of his cocoa face to his pink nose.

Every few hours through the last couple days and nights, I mix up the cow's milk with sweet syrup. Thin it with water. Put it in a baby bottle, halfway to the nippled top. Warm it. Then, out to the lean-to side of the barn, where the colt and Sheba are staying. Settle-down in the heaped-up straw and blankets in the corner. Nestle him in my lap. Say a few Hail Marys—she knows about this kind of thing.

Maybe he even liked it better this way, curled up on the straw, and not having to stand under Sheba's belly searching for her teats. Neither of them seemed to find it easy, him being new to everything and this being her first foaling. She doesn't really seem to mind me taking over. Standing watch at the corner of the lean-to, she munches hay and looks on peacefully.

At first it worked okay—the foal sucked the nipple of the bottle and swallowed the warm milk. But yesterday, he got less and less interested. Today my best girlfriend has come from Seattle by train for a few days' visit, her first summer stay at the ranch. On one side, I'm worried sick about the colt and keeping track of feeding him. On the other, I'm excited she's here.

But Celia, being from a small family in the city, doesn't have the first idea about caring for horses or even feeding babies. We've been best friends since she started high school on the prairie as a boarding student. My mother and hers were best friends in Seattle, before I was born. When she and her parents drove down at the beginning of school last year, it was a big reunion. Since then, we spend time with each other every chance we get. When school was in session, she came over a lot, walking across the big field with me to our house, almost like family. Talking with her, looking into her big eyes, watching the wind catch her wispy hair, everything else almost stops and turns to a fuzzy background. Now she's here at the ranch, and it's summer.

Every time I see her, "My sweetheart," I think to myself and so feel happy about everything.

The air feels too still.

After a quick dinner together and some family volleyball, night comes on. It's the dark of the moon. Celia and I lie in sleeping bags in the back of the old flatbed truck. "Can you hear the crickets? Listen… the owl!"

I do the late-night feeding as Celia waits so as not to startle Sheba and the colt. When I return, meteors are streaking every which way, dripping from one corner of the dark sky to the other. We talk softly. Snuggle, even kiss—the very first time. The night pops with stars and planets.

This is not supposed to be happening.

But I don't say anything, because I don't want it to stop. The wind-up clock tick-ticks in my corner of the truck. Finally, we sleep until the alarm in my sleeping bag rings 2:00 AM.

Careful not to wake her, I rustle up. Jacket on. Into the house. Mix the milk. Warm it. Wrap the terrycloth towel around the bottle and carry it to the colt. My flashlight wakes him in his little corner of straw. My eyes burn. I cradle him. Try to coax the nipple into his mouth. Tip the end up to get the warm milk to drip down. "Come on, little guy. Suck. Suck on it. You can do it."

I think it's going okay, even though he doesn't take it all. The straw smell tickles my nose—sharp and itchy. I sneeze, yawn, finally give up until the next time.

After rinsing the bottle and washing up, I climb onto the flatbed and into the sleeping bag next to Celia. Trying not to wake her, I huddle up close as carefully as I can, hear the small hum of her breathing, catch the scent of her hair. My chest tightens as I look up at the stars, worry about the colt, feel myself caught in the middle of scared, sweet, and confused. Corners of the sky hint that light'll be coming soon. I fall asleep.

But I forget to reset the clock.

Suddenly the bright daylight wakes me. I hear the faraway g-r-o-w-w-w-l  of logging trucks on the road, making their way to the mountains. What time is it?

NO! It's almost 8:00. Daddy's already gone to Mass. I missed the feeding! I race to the kitchen. Mix up and warm the bottle. Where is everybody?

I run to the lean-to. Sheba's not there. Where is she?
In the corner I see the furry colt with his eyes closed. I lift his little head. It's so heavy. Deep in his throat, a hollow rattle. The sticky milk seeps across my thumb and fingers. I clutch the bottle. Salt stings my eyes.

Sheba's hooves are pounding over the dry summer dirt of the upper field. Racing wildly, she circles and re-circles the pasture near the barn. Around and around and around. She snorts. Tosses her head. Cries out a weird, whining cry.

We can't either of us believe it. The cocoa-colored colt is dead.

After breakfast, Celia quietly proposes that she go home early. Later we all gather and bury the colt down the hill from the barn. Mark the grave with rocks and a little cross.

She takes the train to Seattle the next day. We'll make it to see the river and the waterfalls some other time.

*- Dianne Dugaw*

# The Woods

THE BLUE HONDA PULLED INTO THE DRIVEWAY just as the microwave dinged, announcing it was done reheating the coffee he'd reheated yesterday. He could hear them out there, rustling about, but he didn't move; they were accustomed to letting themselves in. He often became lost in thought these mornings, standing at the sink and staring out at the empty bird feeders. Refilling them had been her job.

"Morning, Carl." His daughter-in-law kicked the door closed behind her. She leaned in to kiss the gray wisps on his temple, her glistening dark curls touching his shoulder. "Maya, come kiss your Pop-pop."

The girl came close enough to approximate something hug-like, then walked in-to the next room.

His daughter-in-law caught his look. "Yup, that's still happening."

She rested the girl's backpack on one of the kitchen stools and dropped an aro-matic bag on the counter.

"I brought bagels. And there's freezer bags too, so you can save some for later in the week."

He took his coffee from the microwave's stained carousel and stood there, sipping and staring into his cup. "There's no room in there with all that frozen crap," he said.

She looked for herself. The Tupperware containers appeared to be untouched.

"Carl, people brought these so you'd eat them. Ma would want you to be taking care of yourself."

"I'm fine, for Christsake." He opened the bag on the counter and poked through its contents, pushed it aside. "I don't like onion," he said.

His daughter-in-law looked down at her feet as if she were waiting for him to finish. She did this the last time she stopped by, he remembered.

"You're right. I forgot that. I'm sorry."

She roused herself, circling the room to collect empties, rinsing them out in the sink and dropping them with a clatter into the blue bin by the door. The ashtrays, too, she hunted down and was about to dump them in the wastebasket but thought better of it.

"How's about when Benny gets back he and I come over and help you clear out Mom's closet, and the garage maybe? How's that sound?"

He shrugged at her. He had a high tolerance for disorder, and she was one of those people who couldn't see that as a virtue.

"Guess that's okay," he said. And it was, really. He didn't mind other people picking up after him, if that's how they wanted to spend their time.

He looked at her directly for the first time. "Any idea when that might be? Has he said?"

"Not exactly. Could be a couple of months, which sucks, I have to say." She stared at her daughter in the other room and sighed. "If she's still like this when she starts first grade, I don't know what we'll do."

She took out her keys.

"Anyway ... Thanks for doing me this solid, Carl. The day care's usually reliable but the lady's own kid is sick and I really can't miss any more shifts. I'm sure Maya will love seeing the ... was it a waterfall, you said? Whatever. You sure you two will be OK?"

He sipped his coffee and glanced in the next room, where his granddaughter was tucking some wires into her ears. Her own private sounds, he thought. Every-thing's a big secret with these kids nowadays.

"I did this a hundred times with Benny," he said. "How hard can she be?"

***

The rocks here were more slippery, the patches of moss still shiny with last night's rain. At spots he used the rhododendron branches to tug himself upward, and instructed the girl to do the same. With each step, her pink sneakers lit up, sparkling, as if some energy were transmitted upward from the soil, and the trail's pasty grime began to obscure the cartoon animals that pranced from her heel to her toe. She slipped twice, landing on her knees, but did not complain. He'd promised her a surprise, and that drew her on.

It had been many years since he'd walked in these woods — in any woods, actually. The mix of statins, diuretics, and beta-blockers he choked down daily had served to make him cautious over the years, as if life were fitted with handrails and grab bars. His breath came harder and the pounding in his ears was like a drumbeat — timpani, he thought, isn't that the word for something in your ear? It was in the crossword last week, he was sure. Something to look up later. He used to remember these things.

As the slope steepened, the distance between him and the child grew, and it worried him to see her so far ahead navigating the slick granite, feeling both his duty to help her and his inability to even keep up. He imagined her mother's face if he brought her back bloodied and bruised.

The thought made him stop, and he called to her, "Water break!" Thank God she halted; Benny, all those years ago, wasn't so compliant, but back then he'd been fit enough to chase the boy down.

He unclipped his ancient dark-green canteen from his belt, and she watched, intrigued at this artifact from his army days that he tipped upward, like a bugle in battle. Her own water, sloshing in a complicated sleeve-and-suction-tube contraption attached to her Wonder Woman backpack, the girl left untapped.

She hadn't spoken a word yet. His daughter-in-law had warned him she probably wouldn't. Evidently, it was something to do with Benny's shipping out two months ago. There were some things that kids took harder than us. "Processing" was his daughter-in-law's word for it: the child's subterranean perception of abandonment, or what she interpreted as such. Benny's dereliction of duty — his real duty, that is, not that 20-hour flight to a windblown hellhole on the other side of the world. His real duty, of course, of simply being her father.

He screwed the cap back on the canteen and watched her idly peeling the bark from a rotting trunk that had fallen across the trail.

"That's birch there, in your hand. Good for starting a fire. Bring it here, I'll show you."

She walked it over to him, holding it gingerly as if it were already lit.

He balanced the crinkled sheaf on a rock, away from the other forest litter, and thumbed his lighter. The birch caught immediately and flared white against the granite.

"Pretty cool, huh?"

She looked up, scornful, as if he were some second-rate magician. Her hair was the same dark tangle as her mother's but she had Benny's eyes: quick, challenging. She returned to the log, staring into space, shoulders slumped, to show she could wait till the old coot finally caught his breath. He shook a few drops of water onto the charred birch and screwed the cap back on the canteen.

"Lead on, kid."

Minutes later, up on the ridge, they turned to look back over a sprawling geography: Beyond the pine-needle counterpane they could see roofs, soccer fields, a church spire. Around them the singing of the cicadas grew steadily louder, and he pointed out landmarks and she squinted at them, without comment.

"And that over there, the silvery, shiny line — that's the river. And look, that's the bridge you crossed this morning to get to Pop-pop's house. I used to take your dad fishing on that river."

She didn't react, except to turn around and take a step or two toward where the trail continued into the scrub. But she stopped immediately upon hearing a voice come from that direction.

A black Lab bounded into the small clearing where they stood. It circled them, sniffing at their feet, before it stopped to look back. A tall woman with a long gray braid bouncing between her shoulder blades emerged from the woods. A thin streak of sweat followed her spine down her red blouse. Her knees were swathed in Ace band-ages and a blue plastic bag dangled from her belt like a holster. She stopped mid-trail and leaned on her hiking pole, nodding in turn to both of them.

"You want, you can pet him," she said to the girl. "He's friendly enough."

The dog looked up at the child, as if to confirm this message, and she leaned over, cautious at first but then sitting down so as to be at eye level with the animal. She caressed its head, and it nosed her palm as she did.

He watched his granddaughter pet the dog for a minute, her little hand stroking its muzzle, its cheek, and he felt — childishly, he admitted to himself — almost jealous of their connection. His wife had often touched his own head with such delicacy before that last long, grievous stretch, he recalled. Standing there on the ridge's flinty uplift, he felt his envy was so conspicuous, so discomfiting, that he spoke to divert attention from it.

"We had a Lab once. The wife, she really loved that dog."

"They're the best, aren't they," the woman said. "Love kids. Love the hell out of anyone, is my experience." She pulled a bowl from her backpack and filled it from her water bottle. "Come on, pooch, time to hydrate."

After the dog slurped down some water, it returned to the girl for more nuzzling. The woman took a long drink herself and watched them.

"He sure likes you, hon. You've got a nice way with animals."

The girl stood abruptly, moving away. She kicked a stone, followed it, kicked it again.

He apologized for her. "Sorry, she's a tough crowd. Enjoy your walk."

In another minute, woman and dog were gone, picking their way down the slick rocks that he and the girl had just ascended, and they too resumed their journey.

The trail leveled off almost immediately, and he was grateful for that. Oddly, though, now it was he who led the way. There was some weird law of nature with kids, he thought, a kind of reverse gravity always at work. His son had been the same way: flying up the steep trails and stalling on the flat ones, like snow runoff pooling between hills.

He'd stopped by the night before his flight, Benny had, saying he wanted something of his mom's to take with him on his tour in Afghanistan. The funeral had been only days earlier. The two of them trudged upstairs to the bedroom she and Carl had shared; thet sat next to each other on her side of the bed, cradling boxes of old photos, laughing some, crying too. In the end, the boy took only one thing with him: the little rhinestone pendant he'd bought for her when he was just a kid, which never left his mother's neck until the day the funeral home handed it to Carl in a small manila envelope.

He and the girl walked now through dense clumps of white pine, so thick that their path almost seemed shrouded in twilight. Funny how he didn't remember this part of the trail, he thought. The waterfall was a destination he and Benny had hiked to regularly. Could the forest have changed so much, or was he getting the damned Alzheimer's?

Still, he continued to guide them right or left at various junctions, trusting what he liked to call his inner compass. His wife had always laughed at his claim to such spatial certitude, said her old boyfriends never checked maps either, never would ask for directions. Make my teeth itch, she'd say.

Soon a rippling reached their ears and they crossed a stream on a raft-like log bridge. The sound was almost musical, and they paused to look down into the water. They could see the trees above them reflected there, seeming to grow deep into the muck of the streambed, the branches reaching toward clouds that floated far beneath their feet. The stones embedded there, shiny, could almost be stars or planets. He was deeply moved by this imaginary universe, and he tried to voice its majesty to the girl. She stared at him as he spoke, then bent low over the stream and lay her hand flat against its surface, letting the current divide around her fingers, moving them from side to side like some water strider before letting them dive down and retrieve a smooth black stone, which glistened in her palm.

From here, trail followed stream, and he felt once more sure of his sense of place. But after barely another 100 feet, the two diverged again, and he halted, puzzled. He looked around but the terrain communicated nothing to him. Reluctantly he fished the map from his backpack.

A density of contour lines, whorled like a fingerprint, helped him find the ridge they had crossed. *And there's the parking lot, must be. So, did we follow this stream? Or this one?* Snaky blue lines ran in several directions, and nothing about any of them suggested the route of the tributary they had followed. Nor was there a waterfall indicated anywhere on the map.

Looking up, he noticed the girl was gone. But before he could panic he spotted the bright pink of her backpack at the top of a hill off the trail. He swore quietly and bushwhacked his way to her.

She was standing at the lip of a tufted overhang, looking down into a deep, long rectangular pit faced with limestone and choked with brambles. A thin path cut down-ward through the briars, angling toward the depression's far end, where someone had tented enough fallen trunks across the narrow ravine to create a crude roof. Other tree limbs had been leaned vertically against those to approximate a wall. The whole thing suggested a kind of rough dwell-ing, hidden to view except from this exact spot.

The girl stepped gingerly down the muddy path, sliding in places. Reaching the makeshift bunker, she turned briefly toward him before disappearing behind a screen of bark and leaves.

"Maya!" he called, but she did not emerge, and so he climbed down backwards, spiderlike, unsteady. Reaching the ravine floor, he wiped the mud from his hands and pushed pricker-laden branches aside until he stood at the bramble-framed entrance. He peeled off his pack and ducked inside, into a darkened chamber mottled with slivers of light. Beer cans and a soggy, ragged sleeping bag littered the floor, alongside several large chiseled slabs of limestone. Faint graffiti hieroglyphics embellished one facade, and a knotted, twigged ceiling menaced his scalp.

Dropping her backpack, the child slowly circled the space, lightly touching each wall and the surface of each boulder at her feet. On her face he thought he saw a look of proprietorship, or even more, of a dawning perception, of discovery, like Nancy Drew cracking a mystery.

She held his arm and made him sit on one of the slabs. It was damp, so he first pulled out his nylon jacket to cover the rock. Taking his pack, and her own, she emptied them, item by item, pondering each in turn: canteen, map, sandwiches, baseball cap, thermos, that morning's Boston Globe sports section, a packet of glittery-tipped markers, a thin Magic Schoolbus paperback. She laid these on a chest-high ledge, then turned to stare at him, like he was some problem to be solved.

At last she seemed to have made a decision. Turning back to her supplies, she grabbed the map and unfolded it, draping it over a boulder next to her grandfather. Then she picked up a can from the scuffed soil and placed it on one corner of the map. A dribble's worth of beer or rainwater sloshed around within.

He lay his hand on the map and looked up at her, still not understanding. She turned again, grabbing the newspaper, the paperback, and a marker, then handed him the sports section, folded in quarters. The paperback and marker she held waist high, poised like a stenographer, and looked at him expectantly. Then, she seemed to remember something, and bringing his canteen forward, she mimed pouring something into the beer can before resuming her attentive stance.

He nodded slowly — uh huh, right — and opened his sports section. On one page was a photo of the latest loser that the Red Sox had traded for, and over here, the team standings. Best to ignore those, he thought.

"So," he said, "the pancakes... how are the pancakes today?" He looked at her, waiting for her recommendation.

She narrowed her eyes, and almost imperceptibly shook her head. No, she would not be tricked so easily. He turned a page: soccer scores, yawn. He turned another. Finally he put the newspaper down.

"Well, maybe the eggs, then. Bacon, home fries, the works."

He held the beer can to his lips, feigned a huge gulp, and then pulled out his cigarettes.

"OK to smoke here, Miss?"

She still didn't bite, but he thought he saw somewhere in her face an appreciation for his guile or maybe just his effort. She pivoted to scan the rock shelf, but failing to find a suitable prop, she returned to his table with an imaginary ashtray.

He lit his cigarette and watched his granddaughter at her work. It was pleasant to be waited on, even thus, and he observed the girl's pantomime, interpreting movement after movement: the scrambling of the eggs, the careful separation of bacon strips, the minute adjustment of the stovetop's burners. He tried to remember what it was to move with such purpose. Once, his morning consisted of such chores and the gratification they held: his wife's omelets, her homemade bread, his annotation of the day's honey-do list, the prospect of examining something at his workbench with a doctorly patience, something broken he could make work again.

In a few minutes the girl had finished her labors, and she brought him his meal. He dropped his cigarette into the mud and crushed it under his heel. The eggs, the bacon, the toast, each he savored, chewing slowly, contemplatively, nodding with each bite.

Looking over at her, he saw her gazing out the cave's makeshift entrance, absently twirling the black stone in her hand, looking every bit the waitress daydreaming about her shift's end. He knew she was floating in the heavy hum of the sunlight outside. For some time the woods were still but for the sounds of his dining and the electric chittering of the cicadas.

*- David Desjardins*

# THEN SHE FELL

GENE IS ATTRACCTIVE, NO DOUBT. He has thick wavy hair, and his walk is a little bowlegged, his body settled into his pelvis. Somehow it's sexy. And yet he's kind of repulsive. He walks off the path and sits down on the grass. Sophie follows, careful of her heels, seating herself nearby. Sprawling, Gene gazes into her eyes. He looks like a dog, its tongue lolling out with that little froth of saliva. It's embarrassing to watch. Not even real, certainly not personal, it's all about general fuckability. Which is kind of appalling and kind of exciting in an ass-backward way. Sophie looks away, down at her hand, the fingers open to the close-cropped grass. The Parks Department is on it, she thinks. Sophie works for the city. Straight out of school, she's the assistant to the assistant. Gene works for the governor. That, she supposes, puts her at a disadvantage. He certainly seems pleased with himself, leaning forward on his elbow, his tie lapping at the grass, yearning, or pretending to. He's talking fast, but she isn't really listening. Grinning, he laughs at his own performance. It is funny, and he's bringing her in on the joke. Gene looks like an alligator when he smiles, and Sophie notes that one of his front teeth is chipped. She wonders if he's the kind of man who trades on imperfections. Probably--he has a moustache. Now he pushes back his glasses. He looks so young, like a boy in a business suit. But she recognizes that's part of the seduction. Carefully, she tucks her skirt under her knees.

They're sitting on a swath of grass between the swan boats and the Robert Gould Shaw memorial, the one to the African-American regiment that fought in the Civil War. She loves this park. Though it's lunchtime, neither of them is eating or pretending to eat. They're appraising each other. That doesn't require props. Sophie notices the cadence of Gene's speech; he has some kind of Chicago accent, vowels lagging unexpectedly in the middle of words. Or it could be some kind of speech impediment, that's another explanation. But really, she's feeling shy. Gene's either a wunderkind or a shyster. She knew that much as soon as he tented his fingers on her desk and asked for her number.

"Try my glasses," Gene holds them out. Sophie takes them; she doesn't put them on.

"That's how my parents found out they were perfect for each other: the glasses worked." He smiles.

"An alternative to Cinderella?" Sophie lets the glasses dangle.

"Something like that," he says.

✳✳✳

Ten years later and here she is, on a family vacation in Florida. Her husband, Pete, has arranged it, and Sophie's grateful. Sophie's just turned thirty-two, and she can't remember what it felt like to be herself. First, there was Pete--she kept saying "buried" when she meant to say "married," but she'd done it anyway. She'd resisted anything wifely like laundry or thank-you notes for as long as she could. But now she's fallen into that alternative universe, the motherhood dimension. Morphed, and it's not only her body. Maybe it's the hormones that have tamed her, compliant now. It's not all bad, though, Sophie decides; she's developed a fortitude she'd never had, though she's still a little vague. And of course there's her baby, Arielle.

They're in a huge sports utility, all they could get at the airport. Pete pulls it up in front of the house. The place is arrestingly ugly, cement slabs glued together carelessly surrounded by a moat of asphalt. Is the cement to save money on air conditioning? She ponders the choice. Perhaps she should ask Pete; he's an architect, after all, but he's already out of the SUV. The house looks like something built by Stalin on a road trip to Florida, the concrete slabs perforated by sliding glass doors slatted with metal blinds. There's no green at all, only a paltry row of palm trees running along the side of the property that borders a golf course. She glimpses manicured fairways through the chain-link fence behind the trees. Sophie has never been a golf afficionado. But it's just a four-day trip, and, really, she's glad of it, especially the sun, the warmth. Boston has snow drifts that cover the cars; people are jumping out second story windows and getting skewered on car antennas. She understands the impulse. Arielle is kicking contentedly in her car seat. Sophie turns and unbuckles her, then hesitates.

"Could you carry her?" she calls to her husband.

Pete's taking their suitcases out of the trunk.

"In a minute, babe," he calls. Arielle is fourteen months old and not insubstantial. Jovial and full of beans. "Mam!" She flings out her arms, waiting to be picked up.

"Soon, soon, soon," Sophie pats her leg. Arielle regards her mother, gripping her elephant, Snuffaluffagus, in one hand. She could freak out; for a moment it looks like she will, but instead she starts to sing, "Starsbignliddle," over and over again. It sounds like chirping. If she lifted Arielle and the seat together, it would weigh thirty pounds. Not a good idea as she's in her eighth month. The new baby is stuffed in there, getting bigger every day, and she wants to give him the very best chance—well, of everything. He's breach--nothing to do about that now, though they'd tried EVC. Supposed to be a medical procedure, but really two strong men shoving the baby, butt and head. The baby hadn't budged. Sophie's kind of proud of that. He's sitting inside her cross-legged, a little Buddha waiting to be born. And it should be okay, her doctor says. He'll pull him out by the tail, like a lobster.

Pete puts the bags inside the house. He hauls Arielle and groceries inside, trailed by Sophie, who's carrying the car seat by its handle like a basket.

"Hey!" Gene opens the door. Wearing golf shorts and sneakers with athletic socks, he's still appealing, but less so. An aging boy who's made a lot of money. Grabbing Sophie by the shoulders, he pulls her to him, kissing her on the cheek. Pete puts Arielle down and shakes Gene's hand. Sophie can tell that Gene's a hugger, but her husband is not.

"Who do we have here?" Gene wiggles his eyebrows at Arielle. Arielle hides behind Sophie, pulling on her leggings.

"Don't do that baby," Sophie cups the back of her daughter's head. "Shy," she says.

"She's a beauty," Gene says. She'd forgotten he has dimples.

"Welcome. Was it a tough trip?" Gene's wife joins them. Cathy has a long face and a wide mouth. She smiles now, and her eyes don't change. Sophie wonders how this can be. They'd had drinks once. Cathy wasn't particularly friendly. Sophie remembers a study of surgeons she'd read once. They commit suicide at an unusual rate, but perhaps it didn't include women surgeons. She looks at Cathy's tie-dye top. Sophie'd told Pete she knew Gene from years ago. She'd said from work, which was close enough. Pete had shrugged. Gene was some kind of angel investor now. Pete seemed excited by that; he'd said he liked Gene's energy. They'd met playing squash. Both of them played golf, and they'd decided on the trip. Maybe Gene had suggested it, Sophie speculates.

Cathy seems older than Gene, less attractive, though maybe that's her attitude. Tougher than Gene, that's for sure, and smarter. Marriage is a balance, Sophie thinks. A seesaw, really. Sometimes Sophie loves her husband, and when she doesn't, she counts on the rise. She wonders if it is perhaps Gene's way to dangle women that he had once desired before his wife.

"We're fine," Sophie says, "Just a little tired."

"Hello there," Cathy squats, holding out her hand palm first to the baby. Arielle squats too and doesn't move. Cathy laughs, straightening up.

***

"Can I help?" Cathy asks Pete. He's lined up the perishables he'd brought in from the car. Now he's looking in the fridge like it's a Rubik's cube.

"I got it," he says.

"Do you drink beer?" Gene asks. He points to the door of the fridge.

"Sure we drink beer," Sophie says, though Pete drinks only wine. She sits down at the kitchen table. "It's good for milk production."

"Are you nursing?" Cathy glances at Sophie's breasts.
"No, not anymore."

"Many women enjoy nursing," Cathy remarks. She has no children, but she's a doctor and, as such, an authority on all things pertaining to the body. She knows things, mysterious things. At the bar, Cathy'd told them about the transplants she was doing. Patients in a group they call the 4-H club--hemophiliacs, heroin addicts, Haitians, and homosexuals, and no one knew why they were getting sick. This is a woman who packed in bone marrow by hand.

"Vodka too," Gene says, picking up a bottle. "Clear drinks don't count," he grins.

"Do you smoke? I brought weed," Pete turns to him. This annoys Sophie. First, it's idiotic to fly with contraband, then, what, get arrested carrying a Little Bo Peep shoulder bag? But more important, he's a dad now; he should get it together. It had been fun before, his lack of interest in the burdens of adulthood, but it's getting old. Though he's still remarkably handsome; there's always that. Sophie wonders if he'd managed the renting of this house. She's been so tired lately she hasn't noticed much. It seems like she's always preparing food or going to sleep.

"All right, then," Pete rummages in a cabinet, finds plastic cups and takes out ice. "Anything for you?" He holds up a cup to Sophie, rattling it. This too annoys her.
She shakes her head no.

"Show you the house? We've already moved into our room," Cathy says to Sophie, as if it's an explanation of something. It is, in a way; it explains that they've chosen first. Which is, Sophie thinks, a way to proceed. Not her way, but a possible course of action.

In the living room there's an upright piano. Gene plays, Sophie remembers that. There's a skylight slashed across the vaulted ceiling, nubbly beige furniture with metallic flecks and a large TV.

"The laundry room's upstairs," Cathy says, pointing, "and the master. Let me show you the pool." Sophie picks up Arielle and follows her down a set of stairs. The pool is in the basement. That seems strange for anywhere, but particularly Florida. Black rubber squares tile the room, and the pool itself is narrow, perhaps three lanes. Well, it won't matter; it will delight Arielle. She's an enthusiastic little fish.

***

In the room that is to be their room, Sophie sits. Pete comes in, lugging their bags. He's more relaxed; she can tell from the muscle at the corner of his jaw. In fairness, it's not that easy traveling with a kid, especially if it's yours. Pete opens the suitcase on the bed. He shakes out her two dresses and hangs them up. She is beyond grateful. Then he takes out his own clothes. He is a magnificent folder. Their room is on the ground floor, its sliding doors opening onto the blacktop parking area. Stripping back the coverlet, Sophie finds paisley printed sheets, incongruous in the cultivated neutrality of the room. Perhaps they were on sale. Pete picks up Arielle's travel crib and they set it up together, popping in the quilted mattress. He doesn't stick around while she changes Arielle into her night diaper and pajamas. Arielle squirms fretfully, trying to stay awake. Sophie stands, holding her close, or as close as she can. Arielle's managed to drape herself over the baby bump; her eyes are shutting and her head lolls forward like a wilting flower. The new baby, the one who has yet to make his appearance, slides his head along the curve of Sophie's ribs from the inside. He's playing her like an accordion.

***

It's just beginning to be light, that flat white Floridian light that Sophie associates with stress-filled family vacations. Her parents had favored the state. How has she come to be back here, in this land of strip malls and cluster developments on the edge of a golf course? Sophie looks over at her baby. Arielle sways, gripping the edge of the crib, her feet a little apart for stability. She looks like a tiny pirate on the deck of a ship, watching the curtains ruffle as the fan turns. Motherhood has taken Sophie many places that she would previously have eschewed, and yet she's happy.

Once Arielle's had her rice cereal and Sophie's had her third cup of coffee, they change for the pool. Arielle has a fetching suit with a seahorse on the belly. Sophie believes that maternity clothes are just another way to exploit women's anxieties. She's wearing a black bikini bottom and a T-shirt of Pete's. Kneeling by the pool, Sophie slides on Arielle's floaties. The steps are slippery, and the water is warm. Jets blow soft bubbles from under the lip of the pool. Sophie motorboats her girl around, and Arielle squeals with pleasure as the water hits her belly, trying to dip her head under and taste the bubbles.

"You girls are up early. Nice suit." Gene startles her, looking down at them from the edge of the pool. He has a newspaper tucked under his arm, and he's wearing a Speedo. She doesn't want to look too closely. Sophie pulls down her T-shirt; it's billowed up like a parachute around her body. Her breasts are floating, untethered from gravity. She pulls Arielle close; the baby throws her arms around her mother's neck, covering her chest, and crows.

***

Arielle is napping, and Sophie's sewing up Snuffaluffagus's split seam. The elephant has been destroyed by love. Tiny cross-stiches and brown thread. Sophie concentrates, hoping the repair won't show, that Arielle won't cry that Snuffy has a scar. Across the room she spots an electric outlet she's missed. She'd tried to cover the whole house, the only room she'd missed was Gene and Cathy's. That door had been shut. The pronged plugs come in a bag of twenty; she's still got a couple left.

"I never thought of you as a white picket fence kind of gal," Gene comes in and sits down on the couch next to her. He throws an arm up on the corded back. It's awkward sitting next to him; Sophie feels her weight indenting the couch, inviting him closer. She's gained forty-two pounds, larding it on. It's hard to recognize herself, round-faced with back fat, but she's in there somewhere. The baby too; they're hiding out together. Gene could have sat down on the recliner across from her, Sophie thinks. She wishes he had.

"I'm not a gal," she says. He laughs. It's a belly laugh. She sees that he has a softness in his middle now, a gentle fold. She notices a curl of dark chest hair poking out through the V of his T-shirt. Concentrating, she bends over Snuffy. It's hard to get the seams to line up perfectly; the nap of the fur is worn away. She pinches the sides together.

"Are you going to play golf?" she asks.

"I'm going to watch you sew," he says. Sophie puts the stuffed animal down, sticking the needle into its trunk. The thread trails off like a whisker.

"Strange how things work out," Gene says, and then he's quiet. Sophie sits still. She feels him too close, and yet she doesn't care. "You're popping them out like an animal," he says.

"You don't know anything about me," Sophie says.

Gene shrugs. "Cathy doesn't want kids, I'm fine with that." He starts to drum on the back of the couch with his fingers. It's grating. Sophie starts to sew again. He watches her. She doesn't look at him. Then she pricks her finger, a droplet of blood rises on her fingertip, a bauble, almost decorative.

"Damn!" She pushes off the arm of the couch and stands, the weight of her belly pulls her forward. She sways, then balances.

"Are you okay?" Gene gets up, reaching out a hand.

"Fine," she says. "I'm going to lie down."

"Talk to me," Gene touches her elbow. Sophie hesitates, then sits down on the recliner, raising the footrest.

"You still friends with that guy, David Burke?" Gene's sitting on the edge of the couch. Now he leans back, crossing his legs. "He used to drive you around in that Checker Taxi."

"I don't see him anymore."

"Pete said he came to Arielle's first birthday party. He's the king of med tech." Gene's smile is perfect; his tooth must be capped. Sophie doesn't say anything. "I'm working with a doctor at Mass General, an inventor. He's a diabetic, like Pete."

"How did you know that?" Sophie asks, appalled. Pete hides his diabetes; he won't wear a pump. She doesn't understand his shame, but there it is.

"Squash--he went low," Gene says. "This doctor, his name is Moser, he's invented a way of using islet cells to produce insulin. They float in the abdomen, and they've got one-way doors, so you don't need immunosuppressants." He looks at Sophie expectantly.
"Can you get me in to see Burke? Could be big."

"So that's why we're here," Sophie says. Now she understands why the trip has been arranged.

***

Sophie is lying on the bed in the afternoon heat. She, too, is in amniotic fluid, floating between waking and sleep. She's dreaming of swimming, but then she's underwater, and then she's awake. Looking around for Arielle, she remembers that Pete's watching her. Sophie gets up. She's wearing another undershirt of Pete's. She checks to see that her bra doesn't show through and goes into the living room. Her husband is there in the recliner, hidden by *The Times*.

"Where's Arielle?" Sophie asks.

"Up in their room, Cathy's watching her."
It's then that Gene comes leaping down the stairs, but somehow Cathy's ahead of him. She flings open the front door, racing out.

"Arielle went out the window," Gene says over his shoulder, and then he too is gone. Sophie doesn't understand. The glass doors were shut. Is Arielle outside? Pete runs out. Sophie follows, confused.

Cathy has Arielle pinned to the hood of the SUV, keeping her still. She's feeling the baby's spine. Arielle is making grunting noises.

"She fell on the car. Her spine's okay." Holding an arm straight behind the baby's back, Cathy picks Arielle up. Sophie notices that the hood is dented. Cathy hands the baby to Sophie. It's like a fire alarm has been triggered. Arielle isn't wailing. It's a scream that rises and falls, like something mechanical.

✳✳✳

The pediatrician has been called, the hospital notified. They drive. Sophie is praying, she's making bargains with God, cradling her baby against her body. Please, she begs, and in this moment she believes in God, or at least a universe that can be kind. The baby inside her stirs, and a contraction seizes Sophie's belly, surprising her. She wills herself not to feel. Arielle's still screaming. It's a terrifying sound; the sheer force of it seems impossible. How can this be? The baby's eyes are glazed, and Sophie's blind with fear and rage. Pete says nothing, afraid to look at her. If he weren't driving she'd kill him. Trembling, Sophie kisses the top of Arielle's head. She takes a breath and then she sings, she sings and sings, and then they're at the hospital.

✳✳✳

There's a man standing by the triage station in emergency, his arm wrapped in a bloody shirt.

"Gunshot," he says. The nurse looks up. Arielle is making that siren sound; the room quiets, the man moves aside. Behind the nurse are heavy metal doors. She punches numbers into a pad, and they swing open. The corridor is endless. The doctor is waiting. She places Arielle on the examining table, the thin white paper crinkles. She runs her hands over the baby's body, stopping at the abdomen.

"She fell on her back," Sophie says. Pete comes in from parking. He stands by the door, his hands flaccid by his side. Sophie wonders if he's stoned.

"We'll get a scan," the doctor says. "What does she weigh?" Sophie starts to answer and then bends, the contraction pulling her down. She tries not to groan. The doctor glances at her. "Full-term?" She asks.

"Almost," Pete says.

Holding a hand on Arielle, the doctor pushes a button.

"Let's get you into a room."

The nurse comes in, moving way too fast. Everything is happening too fast. Sophie wants to float away into the ether, to disappear into never, but she has her babies.

"Not yet," Sophie pleads. A technician pushes open the door. Arielle's still screaming. Sophie touches Arielle. Her skin is clammy, and her pupils dilated. She kisses her baby. The man moves Arielle gently onto a gurney. Pete is loitering in the corner, raking back his hair.

"Go with her! Go!" Sophie screams.

***

And then it's over.

"Nothing," the doctor says, coming in. "A contusion on her ankle. Take her to her pediatrician right away." Sophie's lying on a cot. It's cold. The nurse has brought her a light blanket and turned down the lights. "Are you all right?" the doctor asks.

"Braxton-Hicks," Sophie says.

"Hey, it's going to be okay," the doctor says. She touches Sophie's shoulder.

Sophie starts to sob; she feels like she'll never stop.

***

Cathy opens the door.

"Is Arielle all right?" she asks. Sophie nods. She doesn't look at Cathy. She walks to their room and shuts the door. The baby is sleeping, wrapped up in a blanket and dewed with perspiration. Laying her down on the bed, Sophie calls the airline. Pete is in the hall, talking to Gene and Cathy. Sophie doesn't listen to his words. She changes Arielle, strips off her own clothes, and lies down, holding her baby against her skin.

And then it's morning, not even light, before six, but Sophie's up and dressed. When she goes into the kitchen, Gene's already there, scrambling eggs.

"Want eggs?" He turns to her, spatula in hand. Sophie stands transfixed, she can't understand how she's come to be here. She touches her belly, feeling the life inside her.

"Sophie," Gene begins. "The screen--"

"No!" Sophie holds out her hands to block the words. Narrowing her eyes, she stares at him. Gene starts to grow small, until he's almost out of sight. She could erase him with her thumb.

He doesn't look at her. He doesn't speak. Sophie can't see him at all. She turns and leaves. She goes back to their room and shuts the door. Watching the rise and fall of her sleeping baby's belly Sophie feels herself breathe again. She wakes Pete. He wants breakfast but Sophie insists that they leave in the incipient light.

The streets are empty, palms crowning the road. It's an hour to the airport, Pete turns on the radio, soft rock. By the time they get there the terminal is open, beginning to stir. Pete sits in the empty waiting room on an orange plastic seat and reads the paper. Sophie takes Arielle outside, into the warming day. Arielle chatters her sweet nonsense. The baby inside her kicks. Cold in the sun, Sophie understands that she must divorce her husband. It's a matter of when.

***

It will be much later, when Arielle is eleven, that another doctor will look at her MRI scans and ask Sophie if Arielle has ever fallen, and she'll have to say yes. But right now, they're home. Arielle is lying on the changing table, looking out the window from their eighth-floor loft.

"Mama," she says, looking out into the night. "If I fall I'll squish all the buildings."

It will be years before Gene calls Sophie on his fiftieth birthday. He'll say he's calling everyone he thinks he's wronged. He'll ask for her forgiveness. She'll think of hanging up. She'll feel a flicker of recognition.

"No," she'll say.

- Susan Haar

# HYSTERANTHOUS

More than half a life gone before I notice
my neighbor's weeping

cherry, its blossoms splayed across twigs
that silver into nothing at dusk.

And what does it say about blooming, early
or late? Nothing, except that

life always does the only trick it knows,
which is living,

and the cherry forces blooms into raw April,
a canopy of pink stars

in the shape of a tree, shimmering and falling—
the tree waking,

the tree dreaming itself radiant.

*- Kathleen Tibbetts*

# AFTER MATTERS

BEFORE BED, LETTY LIT THE VIRGIN MARY on her altar, touched the blue crystal to her lips, and eased down to her knees to say her prayers in Spanish. Although these days she mostly spoke in English, as there were more gringos than ever living on the border. Letty didn't mind so much; they were, for the most part, respetuoso. Even the newcomers learned to say *gracias*, and most of the Winter Texans mastered *de nada* as well. Letty's Spanish was reserved for private times, or when the English version of a conversation would only serve to confuse gringos who couldn't understand the old ways. Some of the old ways held tight in this high-tech world; not merely because they were traditions, but because they were powerful, *mágico*.

*Mal de ojo.* Letty had been an eyewitness to that curse since childhood. She knew if the spell was caught soon after being inflicted, simple human touch could evaporate it like a trail of smoke from a candle. But if the curse lingered long enough to set its roots, snaking into its victim, a *curandero* would need to be summoned to oust the malice. With words mumbled so low they hummed, the *curandero* would pass a raw egg over the body of the afflicted person, and the egg would absorb the negative energy. That same night, he would tuck the egg, and a cross made of straw, under the poor soul's pillow. In the morning, he would crack the egg and peer into it like a psychic's crystal ball. Then the *curandero* would know if his exorcism had been successful.

This magic had not worked with Fidencio, not on the diabetes or the gangrene. But neither had the gringo's medicine worked. The death certificate indicated sepsis had killed him—her poor husband with no feet. Letty knew this conclusion was only half the truth, but the gringos didn't want to know about the reality of his death—about what she had done.

Tonight, Letty's knees hurt as she prayed at the altar that Fidencio had built for her over fifty years ago. Chunks of missing wood marred the legs where her husband had begun to carve flowers. But soon he had stopped this adornment and announced decorative woodworking was a waste of valuable time. *Suficeientemente Bueno.*

Whenever Fito said this, Letty knew he was finished with the task at hand. She didn't mind the rustic look of the incomplete altar, but she hated that it was too tall, leaving her staring at its edge rather than the

Virgin when she knelt to pray. Many times, she had asked Fito to shorten it, but his reply was always the same, *manana*. So many tomorrows. And at last, *Suficeientemente Bueno.*

Letty finished praying the rosary on her throbbing knees, *Ahora y en la hora de nuestra muerte.* Amen. Then she let Jesus know of her suffering in English because Jesus looked like a gringo to Letty. She was glad Our Lady of Guadalupe wasn't so *blanco.* This was the version of Mary which hung in a gold frame behind her altar, surrounded by a cerulean blue wall, reminding Letty of heaven.

"Oh, my poor, poor knees. My aching back! Jesus, deliver me from my pain."

But Jesus didn't whisper back to her that night, as he sometimes did—as he had that night with Fito eight years ago, advising her how to end his suffering. But tonight, without a heavenly response, Letty conceded her pain was yet meant to be, still a part of God's plan for her. She would ask for a miracle again tomorrow.

Letty held onto the altar and rose to her feet, leading with the good knee, which wasn't so good. She was thirsty from all the praying but didn't dare drink a drop after 7 p.m., or she would be up and down all night. Worse, she might not make it to the toilet. That would be unbearably shameful. Even the thought of this flushed her face.

At last, Letty sat on the bed and carefully positioned her glasses on the nightstand in case she needed to reach for them in the dark. She turned off the lamp before swinging her swollen legs onto the sinking mattress, using a loud groan to fuel this last major muscle movement of the day. As she lay her head on the pillow, she wished *buenas noches* to Fidencio, to whom she always spoke in Spanish.

Fito had protested when Letty studied English soon after they were married. He claimed to speak only Spanish out of loyalty to his ancestors, but Letty suspected parts of his brain didn't work well enough to grasp a second language. She attributed this to his near drowning as a baby in his mother's knapsack. His mother had crossed at Progreso, keeping sight of the bridge. Since the Rio Grande was low that year, she needed to swim only a short distance while clutching her Styrofoam float. As Fito told the story, over and over again, his mother was carrying so much on her back she didn't feel his sack come undone. When she reached the riverbank, she turned to see the drifting baby bundle. Dropping her things, Fito's mother rushed back to save him. Poor Fidencio was floating face-down. It was then the angels carried him back to shore and breathed life into him. Letty wondered if the angels were fellow crossers or border patrol, but she never dared to question the identity, or legal status, of the angels.

Tonight, Letty reached for Fito, as she did each evening. He wasn't where he should be. Instead, she put her hand into a substance the consistency of partially mortared corn. Her first thought was that she had spilled the talc, but she couldn't remember using it anytime recently. The second thought slammed into her, and she bolted up to a sit. Fidencio had been spilled!

"Oh, my Lord, Jesus, no!"

After his death and cremation, Fidencio had not rested even a night in the brass companion urn engraved with both their names. Letty needed him close to her and had emptied the cremains into an oversized Ziploc bag and squeezed out the air. To give him a softer place to rest, she wrapped him into a dish towel and lay him on the pillow next to her own. Letty had intended to make him a better resting pouch, with a zipper to secure him in place. She had gone to the fabric store, even picked out a quilted material printed with angels, baby blue with yellow-gold halos. But while she stood in line for the clerk to cut the fabric, Fito's voice crept into her head.

*¿Por qué estás perdiendo el tiempo en tonterías?*

She didn't know why he thought it was nonsense. Perhaps he was contented resting in a plastic bag. As she contemplated, he spoke again.

*¿No tienes nada mejor que hacer?*

Of course, she had better things to do. There was the gardening, and she hadn't done her dishes since the Meals-on-Wheels woman had brought her food last Friday. Letty could never remember that dear woman's name, so she used an acronym and called her Mow. Three days of dishes waited in the sink covered with a dishcloth to discourage bugs.

Her husband interrupted again. *¿Qué hay de la obra de Dios?* Letty had tried God's work. For years, she had collected food for Our Lady of Perpetual Sorrow's pantry, and each Christmas she picked a family's name from the holy tree and shopped for presents. When school supplies went on sale, she filled a shopping cart with donations for needy school children. Somehow it had all fallen out of her hands after Fito died, and Letty had grown tired of God's work. Besides, Fito hadn't been a particularly religious man; he accompanied her to church only on Christmas. Never on a Sunday. So, Letty wondered why he brought God into the matter of sewing a fitting resting pouch. But she let it be, let him rest for eight years wrapped up in the dishtowel.

Sitting upright in her bed, Letty's heart throbbed in her chest. How could Fito have come undone?

She scrambled for her glasses, but in her angst knocked them to the floor. The lamp listed as she reached for it in the dark, but Letty clutched onto the base with both her shaking hands and finally, shed some light on the situation.

Letty prayed as she retrieved her glasses and eased them onto her face, "Help me, sweet baby Jesus."

There was Fito, all ground up, padded into the sheets, dusting the pillowcase. Her cat Gabby lay stretched out, neck extended, rolling softly into the ashes while playing with shredded bits of plastic bag, her head making a pillow of the dishtowel. Letty's breathing became audible and she waited for chest pains to commence, praying loudly for her salvation between gasps for air.

*"Dios te salve, Maria. Llena eres de gracia."*

Letty's heart raced, but not sufficiently to remove her from this predicament. Her heart slowed. Letty was thirsty, but she didn't dare get a drink. Should she call the kids? How could she explain sleeping with their father's ashes which should have been in a place of honor on the mantle Fito had built from a mesquite tree?

When Fito went to heaven, Letty had made their children promise to mix her ashes with his before planting them both in the garden. It had been Fito's garden, not hers. He had selected the vegetables and herbs, and directed their planting, but held her to the upkeep. Fito had not felt the earth in his fingers or coaxed out weeds or smelled the steaming earth after a long-awaited rain. After he died, Letty planted only catnip and cilantro, which didn't take much tending. For a few years, the tomatoes came, having reseeded themselves, but she didn't much care for tomatoes and left them for the birds.

Letty surveyed the desperate situation. The cat was covered in her husband, as were the sheets. Letty hadn't been making her bed, so the *serape,* bunched up at her feet, had been spared. She needed to save as much of Fidencio as possible. The bedclothes could be rolled up, but she wasn't sure how to detangle her husband from Gabby. Brushing the cat seemed the best option, and she hobbled into the bathroom for the brush. At the sight of it, the cat leapt from the bed, dust poofing into the air like tortilla flour. After several minutes of cautious pursuit— here kitty, here kitty—Gabby scampered out of the cat door.

That part of Fito was gone.

Letty collapsed into her husband's La-Z-Boy. She was in his lap, and he wrapped his arms around her. He whispered she was a good woman. *Muy buena.* He had said that to her on birthdays and mother's days, and sometimes New Year's Eve after tamales, beer, and fireworks. Letty dozed in her husband's embrace, her breathing shallow and heart rate decelerating. It was the next morning when the phone in the pocket of her fire-red and gold embroidered nightdress buzzed loudly. Fito melted, and the chair grew large around her. She had missed the call from her daughter in LA, the girl her husband would frequently proclaim had made something of herself.

*Y nos envía dinero. No nos olvida.*

Maria hadn't always been his favorite, but when his son disappointed him, Fito made a show of exalting his daughter and disparaging Jose. At those times, Letty felt compelled to defend Jose, but she knew better. Fito was looking for a fight that wouldn't end unless she surrendered and agreed (without conviction) that Jose was of no use.

Fito prohibited Letty from phone conversations with her son who, just before graduating from high school, had fled to Guatemala to escape incarceration, flush the drugs, clear his head, and find his path. Jose hadn't intended to become a volcano guide for American tourists, donning an accent that wasn't his. And he hadn't intended to stay on and on. He stayed even after Fito became ill, even after Fito's construction business, built from nothing, had to be sold well under-market. With no family to run the family business, Fito lost his legacy.

Letty knew her daughter would call back. She moved to the living room where she could admire the picture of Maria in her graduation gown as they talked. She stroked the glass, placed the phone on her lap and waited.

Maria's love was organized, practical, and prompt. She called Letty every day on her lunch break; asked what her mother was doing, what she had eaten, and what she planned to eat for dinner. As much as Letty found this part of the conversation tedious, she loved what came next. When it was Maria's turn to tell, she would talk about work. Litigation, arbitration, defamation, habeas corpus. Letty kept a growing vocabulary list on the side table. She didn't care so much what it all meant; what she loved was hearing the energy and passion in her daughter's voice. Letty picked up the buzzing phone.

"You okay *Mamá?* You didn't answer, and I got worried."

"Yes, *mija.* I only was asleep."

Without waiting for Maria's interrogation, Letty reported she had huevos rancheros for breakfast and planned to make chicken flautas for supper. But neither was true. How could she eat with Fito scattered about the house? Maybe toast later and Salisbury steak with potatoes and gravy from the Meals on Wheels lady. She hadn't decided.

"But tell me of your day, Mija."

"*Mamá*, the judge was hysterical this morning. She threw some guy out of the courtroom for smacking his gum too loud! Told him to chew his cud in the field with the cows. Then the judge said it was the most disgusting habit on earth. I could have peed my pants Mamá."

Letty laughed with Maria, but her heart ached with longing. She didn't dare ask Maria to come home and help with the mess Gabby had created, but she missed her daughter.

"Are you sure you're okay Mamá?"

"Just missing your Papá today."

After the call, Letty rolled the sheets tightly together, bound them with kitchen twine, and placed them in a plastic trash bag. She squeezing out the air, tied the end, and put the bag into her most beautiful flowered pillowcase. Letty remade her bed, laid the Fito pillow next to her own, and climbed in next to her husband. The cat joined Letty in the bed and repeatedly flopped on top of Fito, liking the muffled crunch of the plastic bag beneath before kneading it into her resting place.

"Oh Gabby, what trouble you have made for us."

Letty gently massaged the cat's forehead with her fingertips, and the cat purred music into Letty's dreams of her husband. But it was the angry man dreams that came to Letty that night. Fito was red in the face, teetering on his stumps, shaking his finger, and accusing her of desecrating his remains. Worse yet, he shouted at Letty about her unkept promise.

*¡No hiciste lo que prometiste!*

When she woke, Letty tried to explain she couldn't have kept that promise; it was a mortal sin. But she knew Fito would never let her rest in peace.

Because Gabby had scattered tiny bone fragments and dust particles everywhere in the house, Letty couldn't bring herself to vacuum or mop. She knew the AC was circulating Fito, knew she was breathing in tiny particles of him. And Letty couldn't be sure if it was ordinary dust, or Fito, in the spaces between the floorboards, so she didn't sweep either. She walked softly around the old house in her socks and didn't wash them. Instead, Letty put them in a wicker basket under her altar with as much reverence as she could give worn socks.

In another three weeks, Letty was out of socks. When she

shopped for them at the dollar store, she also purchased a zippered pillowcase and put it under the one with the purple flowers. After the shredding incident, Letty didn't trust Gabby and wondered why, after so many years, the cat had attacked Fito.

Gabby and Fito had gotten along well when she was a kitten, but after a year, Gabby began to hiss at him and run from him. This change in her behavior came immediately after Fito told Letty the cat broke her leg falling from the mesquite tree. He had wrapped Gabby's leg between two halves of a paint stick, los animales mejoran o no – because didn't believe in doctors for pets. When Letty noticed the claw marks etched into the backs of Fito's hands, she prepared a calendula salve for them both. Each night she circled the blue healing crystal over Gabby's body until the cat could no longer be caught. At least, she thought, the shiny stone worked well on animals. Fito wasn't convinced the crystal could cure anything, but he wouldn't risk offending it, so about that, he stayed quiet.

After the doctors took his feet, Fito didn't believe in doctors for people either. Finally, he allowed the hospice nurses into the house to check his vitals and change the sheets, but he wouldn't see a doctor. His moaning increased in volume whenever the nurses were present, and they gave him the sympathy he desired. Letty was grateful as her own empathic responses had diminished considerably, despite her efforts to emulate the Blessed Mother.

The nurses also left comfort kits, which included liquid morphine, morphine suppositories, and medications for nausea and constipation, but Fito didn't want the gringo's medication. Still, he told Letty to collect the kits in case he someday couldn't manage the pain on his own. This was one of the few times Letty deceived her husband. When Fito would be out of his head with stomach pain, she made strong herbal tea, which took away his suffering and helped him sleep. He was used to her bitter teas and tinctures, the Bricklebush, Eucalyptus, and Malabar, which were supposed to cure his diabetes, but hadn't. Then came the night Jesus told her what to do. As she did each night, Letty had served Fito tea and his pain had abated. She watched him grow relaxed and tired and waited for his eyes to close. But that night he called her to his side, telling Letty to bring the chair and sit next to the bed. She brought her crucifix as well and rubbed the dying Christ as Fito spoke.

*Quiero que camines al cielo conmigo.*

He told her they should be together, that she should walk with him to heaven. Letty agreed, *Sí*. Someday she would. Letty could see the tea was making him drowsy because the ever-present creases between his eyes softened. His eyes grew glassy but remained open and fixed.

*La morfina de los kits, ¿dónde está?* His voice was suddenly urgent.

Letty told Fito she had saved the morphine as he wished, but in reality, she had only saved the suppositories. The herbal tea had been mixed with the liquid morphine each night. Fito told her he was tired of the pain and was ready to die. She nodded as he continued.

*Moriremos juntos, como Romeo y Julieta.*

This time Letty didn't say *Sí.* How could he ask her to die with him, to hasten his death and take her own life? Had the sickness deranged his mind? Perhaps she had been giving him too much morphine.

Letty shook her head. No Fito, no es possible. Dios no…
He did not let her finish, did not give her time to explain that God would not permit suicide, and she would go to hell if she took his life or her own. Fito tried to raise his voice but instead set off a raspy coughing episode. Letty trembled as he continued to speak through sputtering, hacking, and gagging, telling Letty they should die together, demanding she promise to drink the morphine with him.

*Prometeme! Tu propósito es estar conmigo.*

Letty felt his barbed words piercing her tired heart. Did Fidencio really believe she had no purpose on earth outside of caring for him? She dropped the cross onto her lap and reached for Fito, but he pushed her hands away and grunted.

There were so many times she had reluctantly acquiesced to her husband's wishes. She had obeyed when he told her school was a stupid waste of time, when he said she could not go to Mexico to visit relatives, could not buy clothes she wanted, and could not have friends over. And even when he told her to work as a cleaning lady for the gringos after Jose and Maria had left home. Still, Letty knew he was a good man. Fito had never hit her. He had provided for his children, and she had a beautiful home. Her life was good.

With her hand covering her mouth, she promised to walk with Fito to heaven. *Sí prometo.*

That night Letty heard from her savior while kneeling at her alter. Jesus had whispered, in English, it was time to help Fito out of his pain. Letty understood and made the sign of the cross in acknowledgment, touching her head, then her chest, her left shoulder, then her right. At the kitchen sink, Letty soaked and steeped the morphine suppositories, adding Bricklebush tea leaves. Then she poured the hot mix into a mason jar and placed it outside for the morning sun to cook. Early the next evening, she strained the liquid through cheesecloth, poured it into a Talavera pitcher, and sweetened it with honey.

When Fito told Letty it was time for them to go to God because his pain was unbearable, she brought two cups of tea and sat beside him in the chair. She promised they would walk to heaven together. As they drank, Letty prayed the rosary, moving a bead with her thumb for each recited Hail Mary and Our Father. Fito went to heaven alone that night, but Letty held his hand until his dying breath and finished praying the rosary.

*Te amo, mi esposo.* Then she apologized for her falsehood and vowed to join him when it was God's plan for her. It wasn't her time. She hoped he would understand this now that he was with Jesus.

But even after these eight solitary years, she knew he hadn't forgiven her. No matter how she tried to explain and apologize, it was his angry face she saw each night when she closed her eyes. It followed her relentlessly.

The night the chest pains came, Letty lay her head on Fidencio in the pillow and wrapped her silver-beaded rosary around her hand. She prayed until her heart imploded, "Voy a venir Fito." Her body vomited bile onto the pillow, and she peed her bed, but she didn't know these things. Gabby moved to sleep above Letty's head and play with her hair.

***

After Matters.

It was Mow, the Meals-on-Wheels lady, who discovered Letty the next morning. She had found many of the expired elderly in her dozen-plus years as a volunteer. These days she didn't rush to make the 9-1-1 call. She checked for a pulse, but it wasn't necessary. Mow recognized death. She bowed her head and prayed the Our Father. Then Mow looked for a memento. She knew the family wouldn't give her a thought, wouldn't recognize she had been a comforting presence for years. Mow wouldn't take anything valuable; she never did. She wasn't a thief and only sought a remembrance, a token and reminder. She thought about unwinding the rosary from Letty's hand but went instead to the altar.

The blue crystal lay at the feet of the Virgin Mary statue. Mow slipped it into her pocket. It would look beautiful on her altar, and she would pray for Letty's soul every night–like she did the others, in case they were doing time in purgatory. She was attending to death's after matter.

The remains of Fidencio's cremains, unfortunately, found their way to the county dump—still in the plastic garbage bag with the rolled sheets zippered in a cloth bag, and topped with the pillowcase of purple flowers covered in dried bile. But that was not all of him. When the cat left the house covered in Fito, she went to the garden and rolled in the catnip Letty had planted. Which is exactly where Maria and Jose scattered their mother's ashes as they said their prayers—in Spanish.

*- Noreen Graf*

# To posterity

Future life – that vaulted marble manse
With capillary eyes full of silver
Want, more than all elevated type
Of want, is just slight dust, one smallest pile
On endless tile, the blood-flat volumes
In even flux – its inborn animal
Recalled would kill – the sound, metallic,
Singular, no human speech could copy –
The printed page's other language –

On that we'd write a letter,
Self-sent and self-received –
Our two natures on the day
We won't compare
Which we compare, compare:

*To posterity,*

*Misprinted name, our black century*
*Like nightshade on night's field,*
*Where one can't tell if the dome is open*
*Sky, nor ocean-hidden places beneath*
*With sex animated, populated*
*In skirts of dark thought, kissing colder lips*
*As they breathe grey and green –*
*Emerald and diamond-deep evening's*

*Creative waters, warm to the morning*
*Summer, skinny, straight – they're dancing on sand*
*For the tired judge – desire doesn't age,*
*But grows younger, eyes too wide in their youth –*
*The evidence of sight, his bright sees him*
*Seeing and that undocumented life*
*To come, seafaring o'er its broken face*
*A nonsurface of space for none above*
*Now in flattest blue days, nor any*
*Coming human race's wetted colors.*

Signed,

Your lightest lover

*- Alex Van Huynh*

# MY BRIEF AND TUMULTUOUS LIFE WITH K

DURING DAYLIGHT HOURS WE SHOPLIFTED packets of cheese from mom-and-pop stores. In the cover of darkness we pinched apples from a nearby orchard. Our hunger was never quenched.

Back then, before the climate changed, the rains were relentless. Mudslides were common along the twisty roads of northwest California. Redwood trees fell across the main highway that led to the moldy cabin we rented near the town of Bridgeville. I split the smaller rounds of redwood for firewood. I knew it was wrong to burn up such glorious old growth trees but we needed the warmth.

The Van Duzen River ran high out the back door. Salmon swarmed in the pools, then died and rotted on the banks. That winter the dogs got into porcupines. I held them down, made them swallow aspirin, and pulled the quills from their soft noses with pliers. A few days later the dogs found the porcupines again.

K, the woman I lived with, set up a darkroom. She took black-and-white photos of me nude, in various arty positions, then developed the prints and hung them to dry on a makeshift clothesline. She rolled her own cigarettes and filled them with Drum tobacco. She did crosswords and chain-read Dick Francis mysteries.

She drank too much, but I was too young and horny to care. We were unemployed, living on fanciful lies, borrowed money, and pawnshop exchanges. I don't remember what the goal was or even if we had one. The future held no meaning. We were on a downward spiral, inhabiting a Raymond Carver short story of desperation and drunkenness. It got nasty.

K, who was three years older than me, had a beautiful singing voice. She loved Hoyt Axton ballads. She would sing them in public, in cafes and restaurants. Sometimes people would clap. I eventually found it embarrassing.

We met while working at a liquor store in a tourist town in southwestern Colorado. K would steal bottles of wine and we would drive up into the mountains and get drunk.

K's life was tragic. She was raped at gunpoint in Los Angeles. The rapist was never found. She later saw him on the streets of her neighborhood. At another liquor store where she worked, this one in Santa Fe, she was held up and ordered to fetch the robber a six-pack of beer. She returned with Budweiser. "No," he demanded, "I want Coors!"

She laughed in his face. He ran off without any beer or money.

K had been in a terrible car accident. A scar ran the length of her face across her nose, but it did not diminish her beauty. She had let a Navajo kid drive her Karmann Ghia and he could not negotiate the canyon curves of New Mexico. They were probably drunk. The car was totaled. She was hospitalized for months. I never learned what happened to the Navajo kid.

She could afford to make mistakes. Her parents were wealthy. They lived in Pacific Palisades, an uber-rich neighborhood in southern California. We stayed with them once. I didn't know how to talk to them, so I mostly hid out in the guest room and noodled on my guitar. K spent a day with an old boyfriend.

Aside from her black hair and blue eyes, it was K's sadness that attracted me to her. I foolishly believed I could cure her sorrow. My immature clinginess, my belief that I could make her happy, coupled with the constant coastal fog and cold drizzle, only contributed to her misery. We were doomed to fail as soon as we met.

Before we found the cabin in the woods we lived with our dogs like vagrants. We slept rough outside or in the big pink station wagon K bought off a friend of mine in Colorado, where K and I met, and where she told me of a "magical" place of redwoods, banana slugs, and ocean tides. She said it rained all the time so I packed up my few belongings and took off with her.

When we first hit the North Coast and drove through the fog it gave me such a faraway, dream-like sensation. The Feeling lasted all the way down to the Trinidad's little bay and harbor.

I kept saying to K, "I want to live here! I want to live here!" So romantic with the fishing boats bobbing on the water, the crab traps piled like cages alongside the dock. Starfish clinging to rocks. We stopped at the Seascape Café and drank liebfraumilch and nibbled on oyster crackers, biting off the corners of the crackers to form various US states. K sang me the 'East Virginia Blues.' The night was blue and dark. Seals barked. The wind picked up. We slept in the sand to awaken to a wet, cloudy dawn.

We also awoke to a broken car window. My guitar, K's dulcimer, and an unopened bottle of gin were stolen. Miraculously, I later found the guitar displayed in a store window in a music store in Eureka. We never did find the dulcimer. We quickly replaced the bottle of gin.

I was twenty-one years old. K was twenty-four, but she seemed even older. Today's New Age vernacular would call her an old soul. She took pottery classes at a nearby community college, an hour from the cabin. I took a sign language course, then a sheep-shearing workshop. Nothing seemed to stick.

Of course we would break up. It got violent, mostly verbally, but the cloud of physical violence had moved in. I'm not proud of my part in any of it.

After K split, she lived for awhile with two gay women in a Victorian house in Eureka. I remember the last time I saw her. I had brought over her pottery wheel. She was happier, full of energy and not weighed down by my neediness. Her roommates were not friendly. It was terribly awkward.

Years passed and I moved on through several relationships and one divorce. One day out of curiosity I searched for her online. An obituary from the Kansas City Star popped up from 2018. K had died from cancer the age of 64. There was a black-and-white photo, her head tilted with her alluring smile and mirthful eyes. She had married, raised two daughters, was a Missouri Master Naturalist known as the Snake Lady. The obituary read, "Her strength and fortitude were only belied by her infectious laugh and kind heart." She went on to discover what she was always looking for: a stable partner and love.

It felt so intrusive to do so, to be the typical internet voyeur, but I could not help myself. I searched for her last address, for images of her daughters and husband on Facebook, to try to fill out the life she had lived after me.

The daughters and her husband would know little, if anything about the times we spent on the North Coast. About the shoplifting, the dogs, the drinking, the desperation. Perhaps they came across those nude photos in her belongings. Maybe K told them things about me that I would have wanted to keep secret. Still, the fact remains: I knew K long before they knew her.

Did she ever search for me? Did she find that my life stabilized? That I finished my degree, raised my own daughter, finally married wisely, wrote five books, and grew into my better self?

K's and my life intersected at a time when we both were searching for something that we could not name. Eventually we both found it, but with different partners. Yet, for a couple of intense years we were *everything* to each other. That was also part of K's life, whether her family knows it or not. I did mean something to her once. She would write love notes to me in my journal. Cook me incredible omelets filled with ranch dressing, green onions and mushrooms. Accompany me on my guitar with her strong melodic voice. Patiently show me how to please her in bed and, in turn, I held her during those nightmarish nights when the memory of the rapist woke her. I am most proud of those moments.

How do you purge past relationships when they cover you permanently like tattoos? When they seep and settle forever into the pores of your skin? When it is too late to take back the words you said, both in anger and even in tenderness?

All I've learned is that so much of one's existence is temporary. But I didn't learn this lesson until much later in life, when I began to sift through my past instead of looking forward toward my diminishing future.

And always when it was too late.

*- Stephen Lyons*

# THE LIGHT IN YOUR MOUTH

After a line by Marvin Bell<br>After a line by Theodore Roethke

Joy to be wordless yet wide awake
following the light
in your mouth
you breathe slowly on a mirror
until vapor clings
to the image bent over
the dark it can't help
but resemble after all
being awake is familiar
passed down through mutations
hurled out of the dawn
somehow the day builds
against the edge of Earth
never revealing the crack
where it slips
past the tongue
the source
you remember
the lilt of sparks
going round the bonfire
denied the darkness
you held out
for inspection

- Gregory Jensen

# THE STONE WOMAN GETS UP DANCING

Song of the Precious Mirror Samadhi
by Dongshan Liagjie

The void of you swells and numbs
like anesthesia before a filling

nothing is possible since

you ended, the edges of you so easily erased
leaving me sealed in suspended time

I wear my story like a black armband
or a winter coat made of stone

*We interrupt your grief to announce the first yellow crocus*
*was sighted at the corner of Melrose and Madison*

who am I without a mother who couldn't
my rage wrapped like a worn sweater

touching bruises and scars over and over
the way a tongue settles on a sore tooth

a hotline dialed at midnight
*what is your address? hello! hello!*

*We interrupt your rage to watch moonlight*
*swaying muslin curtains in a wide window*

I think maybe life isn't for everyone

I hear an undersong stirring
unlocking loss, softening betrayals

who will I be without the hard crust of habit
without static stories and unshed tears

who will I be when the stone woman gets up dancing
skirts flaring, bare legs flashing

I reach for the familiar, dark and songless
afraid to let myself happen again


*- claire scott*

80

# Catacombs

Planetary oval lights transmigrating through pools of ether. Ash domes, a whippoorwill trilling. There in an unpacked room a millennium of stars passengers of bluish light. A nod of opaque sapphire where autonomous creatures smirk and tread through memories. They laugh like children in a grizzly manner because life placed itself auspiciously in their laps. There is seldom a reason to think people in passenger trains or passing strangers have not lived such an easy life as the one you are living. Cars tressed with Indian food, a kiss on the hip then to the pocket of skin near the stomach and elsewhere like travel around towns where you collect names: beads of amethyst or amnesia, waking or sleeping, wandering or idle, a tidal wave between the legs may bring a foreboding transit of books from one shelf to another, a slow escape of indescribable words; they sleepwalk along catacombs. At bedtime hands unclasp and mirrors are sapped of their own music, a furnace of books collecting heat: wise words rise from rosy lips saturated with cold sweat. But this was the end as well as what you mentioned of a beginning in passing.

*- Harry Palacio*

# Deadheading

"HIS NAME'S CLIVE. Clive Hortener, and he's even weirder than his name."

Emma nods and takes a bite of the hamburger I bought her. We meet at McDonalds. I know it's not the cool place, but since I'm only fourteen and can't date yet, we have to find a place close to our houses where we can just *run into each other.*

"How long have you worked for him?" she asks.

"Just this summer. He's been my neighbor forever but when I was growing up he didn't talk to me except to tell me to quit shooting hoops so close to his flowers."

"So, what do you do for him?"

"Ah, you know. Weed the flowers and vegetables, haul mulch, cut limbs, rake stuff up. He tells me what he wants and he's usually right there showing me how, as if I couldn't figure it out."

She nods.

"I'd like the job a lot better if he'd just tell me what to do and then leave, but he hangs around and talks and talks. Mom says he's just lonely because his wife died, but he talks about weird things."

I chew on my burger while Emma runs her tongue over her braces to make sure all the food is out. Then she moves her knee closer to mine until it's almost touching.

I want to say more. This is a casual conversation, but I don't want it to be casual. I want to tell her about the time Clive caught my wrist in the tree loppers when he was pruning. I want to tell her how my stomach clenched when he laughed and said, "You know, I could take your hand right off." I can't tell her what I saw in those watery eyes set in that old melting-skin face, because the only word I can think of is scary and that's a little kid's word.

"You ever hear of blood meal," I ask suddenly.

Emma shakes her head.

"It's fertilizer stuff. It comes in a package and it's actually dried blood."

"Come on," she half laughs. "I don't believe that."

"But it's true. It really is. When Clive told me it was blood, I didn't believe him either, but he showed me on the package. You can buy it in gardening stores."

"Gross," Emma says. "That's really disgusting."

"Yeah, and when Clive put it on his squash and lettuce he said maybe it wasn't just *animal* blood."

"He is weird," she says dipping a French fry into ketchup.

"True story," I confirm. "And there's a fertilizer called bone meal which is made from ground up bones."

Emma makes a gagging sound.

"Yeah, and he has me put that on his carrots and onions," I continue. "And while I'm doing that he's talking to me about what his wife used to cook for him, people he thinks are trying to ruin the country and people in the neighborhood he doesn't like. He seems to know something bad about everyone on my street and I don't know whether to believe him or not. I keep thinking, *how could I not know that*? But then I wonder if he knows that or he's just making stuff up."

Emma chews thoughtfully, not saying anything—but she's listening.

"And he talks about Russia controlling our computers and how bad politicians are corrupting our minds and how Trump is going to lead us into another war and I'm going to be drafted and blown to bits."

"Wow!" Emma says. "I wouldn't want to work for him."

"I don't either but how dumb does it sound to tell my parents I quit my summer job because the guy scares the crap out of me?"

"You could look for another job," she says. "But I guess you can't tell him what to talk about when it's his yard."

I nod. *She is listening* and it makes me feel warm and special.

"Clive likes flowers," I continue. "And even though it seems like he doesn't like people,  he compares them to flowers. He'll talk about how pretty roses are and yet they're out to get you with their thorns. He says that's how people are. And when some of his tulip bulbs die and don't come up the next year, he tells me most people are like that. You can't count on them to be there for you. I don't know why he grows flowers."

"Maybe so he can complain?" Emma volunteers.

I grin while asking, "Do you know what deadheading is?"

Emma shakes her head.

"Once roses or some other flowers have bloomed, they need to be cut back, so the next flowers can bloom. So, you cut the flower off to make way for the next one. And Clive says some people need to be deadheaded to make room for others with better ideas."

Emma finishes her burger and takes a drink of her soda, but she says nothing.

I crumple my wrapper. "Doesn't that sound kind of weird?" I press. "You don't figure maybe he'd deadhead people, do you?"

Emma looks surprised. "But he's old, right? I mean he's not going to go into some school and shoot people, right?"

I nod, "Yeah, he's really old."

"Well, then," Emma says tossing her silky hair and looking up at me with her sparking eyes. "There's nothing to worry about, other than being bored to death by all that talking, right?"

I nod. She listened to me and heard me out. She's right, I guess. Maybe he's not a threat, but I still don't want to work for him.  But like Emma said, I can look for another job. I'm not stuck with him.

And then tonight, I'm watching the follow-up news about the shooting in Las Vegas, and the guy on TV says, "The shooter is reported to be Steven Paddock, a 64-year-old man living in Reno." Really? Sixty-four! Not as old as Clive, but still. . .

*-Lorraine Jeffery*

# Bleached Bones

TERRY MUST KNOW BEST, waving away information centre guide-books, whispering, 'they're rip-offs.'

Since their earliest email, Sue called him The National Geographic. Always mouthing greater knowledge. Particularly local flora, fauna, environmental issues and wilderness expeditions. Coming across as an agitated David Attenborough.

Hushed people filled gallery space behind the information centre lobby, awe struck by huge landscape photographs, paying reverence as if these images were memorials. Yet Terry walked around uttering barely suppressed irritation.

On the trails Terry dropped his constant light touches on her elbow. Stopped asking, 'you ok. Not too much?'

Difficult walk, this trail; climbing long, steep inclines with a pack on, into fierce winds. A lot more difficult than Sue had anticipated. But chilled September air, forced her to think of lost first peoples. As fellow walkers slogged up an incline overshadowed by Crater Lake Tasmania, steep canyon walls, her pack morphed into bricks, all sharp edges.

Straps rubbed her shoulders too, foreboding chaffing.

By mid-afternoon, they encountered light drizzle. Rather than soak in, moisture sat on surfaces and gave everything a damp smell.

This walk had started in tussocky grass. Later she found seeds trying to plant themselves in her socks, even breaking through to tender skin. A mere scratchy twitch compared to grief of original inhabitants of these lands.

Small things drew her attention; how snow gums wore patterns, a bark patchwork, largely flame shapes. A creek tinkling off in a nearby gully, cicada hums, light twittering from some invisible bird. Smells of burnt nutmeg, lemon tinged.

Further, along the trail they passed some bushfire damage; pale almost colourless windswept grass, craggy rocks and dead trees sticking out like skeletal fingers. A landscape corpse with no flesh, just bare bones, left behind. Tree trunks completely bare and bleached white by sun's glare through this thin mountain air.

Haloed in sun, walkers rested beside a tiny stream. Finally, able to take their shoes off. White toes might be mistaken for grubs wriggled about in icy water. This breather felt so good.

Walking again, she peered up at a track, forming a scar. Other brightly clad walkers strung out, made tiny by vistas. Sue experienced a sensation akin to dropping into a calendar. No, more like a giant frieze.

Up at the lookout, Sue gazed out over views rolling off to a vanishing point beyond lake edges far below. She felt dizzy, slightly high. Sky pressed down and ground pressed up, jamming her between like a tiny speck. No, a minuscule troublesome piece of dust.

When she looked down Sue felt she could step off this fragmented rock edge and bounce downward like a pearl gestating speck. A weird momentary desire to jump brushed against her. How would it feel? Not clean, like bungy jumping leaps off buildings or bridges, swan diving through empty air, nor shades of 9/11 falling man images. She pitied decisions to select death.

Looking up at spines of rock-ringed crater above, Sue imagined a dragon's backbone.

Stunted trees appeared in pain. Wind, snow and storms must weigh them down like Sue's pack did. Yet leaves and bark embodied strength and solidarity.

She felt defeated but knew it would be wrong to give up, cede before really beginning her grand adventure.

'We'll go do the Overland Track,' Terry had suggested, months ago.

'That's four days, walking, in mountains. I don't … well I'm not so used to country.'

'It will be epic,' He insisted.

Too daring, too physical, but now her efforts headed toward worthwhile. A catalyst forcing Terry to fade fast. Not even worth a thought compared to hot tingles in Sue's nerve ends, synonymous with new growth. This landscape and air impressed way beyond any human, dead or alive.

She paused to take in breathless hushes. Listen to wind, and plot connections with her own slushing breath. In her mind, Terry kept reducing, nothing more than another mere human walking clearly gouged trails through this majesty.

Early that morning they'd argued. She'd threatened to wander off, alone. Sue wanted to – but knew how stupid this idea. They'd paid money to do an organized trek. Being lost up here, was beyond imagination. Stumbling through shrubs, tripping on rocks, yelling at un-answering emptiness. Why would she? Dumb to stumble into uncharted shrub, to push through thick brush, scratches on arms and legs, to encounter that sinking panic at not being able to identify locations of tracks. Any signs of humanity quickly vanished, consumed by bush. No wonder escaped convicts stooped to cannibalism, or preferred returning to their cells, suffering punishments rather than stay, alone, trapped out here. Trees, scrawny beside trail edges, fringed with unexpected sinister broodiness. Yet beautiful enough to make her skin tingle more.

Alone in her tent, Terry missing, she heard gurgling, scary threats invisible to humans. Sounds guides reassured came from possums or Tasmanian devils. Sue thought of these noisemakers as scavengers, ghosts, or ghouls, embodying perfect attendants for Terry. Now vanished, he obviously preferred dark corners alive with these scratching to her company.

Someone, she didn't know for sure who, some youngster on work experience planting trees, maybe a chronic unemployed person working for benefits by repairing trails, or a farmer, perhaps another walker or one of those sticky-nosed uniformed types would eventually find Terry's bleached bones. By then Sue's presence, no more than eucalypt haze or blurred photographs, would fade from memory. Her presence merely gone.

*-Karen Lethlean*

# Jimmy Olsen

Why perhaps as mundane as the shared last name—
life no doubt different if born Ivanoff or Carlson.

But I'm not alone: there's an army of Jimmies
(and Janies) out there just like me.

Always the ones in pratfall, needing rescue, never
the names in all caps gracing the cover.

Sidekick, pal, wingman. The wannabe who loses himself
in a cave, gets stung by radioactive bedbug.

The BFF with the faulty camera used as bait
to ambush the dim but dashing hero. Object, not subject.

Superpower, if any, magnified neediness, garnished
with a soupçon of envy. But given the choice,

be honest, would we have it any other way?
Like the child at a wedding banquet

tossed in the air higher and higher by a tipsy uncle,
the thrill of being caught, the thrill of not.

- Kurt Olsson

# Ave, Verum Corpus

Sitting on my doorstep this Sunday afternoon
while my daughter beats her father
a second time at Mancala, I see a baby lizard
gumdrop green by my feet. Moving
only its paintbrush head, the slender torso remains still
like the red brick canvas
holding us both.

A text from my mother— My
heart bursts with love for you. I can physically
feel it. And my cats stand watch
in the window, linked to the lizard's every twitch.
Only now it is brown. I Google why

do lizards change colors and learn this tiny guy
is an anole who turns brown
from stress or fright. I blame my husband
who protests his third loss at Mancala, but he points
at our domestic short hairs silent
as spider-silk, watching their prey
scurry up the wall. Love

bombing is something else I recently learned
about. It's the narcissistic mother's gambit
in a cycle of manipulation. It almost
always results in a victory. I notice
the lizard is again green
as my daughter counts the glass stones, closing
her wooden case like the eyelids
of a small animal. Can I drive down
and visit you this summer, my mother texts.

I fall for it. Sure!— and she drops her stones
one by one into the divots
of my inner child. I turn brown. Or you could
drive up here, you know.

*- Candice Kelsey*

# THE GROUND BENEATH US

THE HOUSE HAD BEEN SINKING for some time—fourteen years at least, though perhaps longer. Anyone could've seen the place couldn't last: one haphazard, wooden house in the center of a swamp, two hours from the nearest town, built first by our father to be a fisherman's hut, then expanded messily upward as a home for two, three, then four, then three again. The squat trees holding our house above the water simply could not bear the weight of a second floor.

Our father believed the house would settle with time. He added small spears of wood that sank deep down into the silt beneath the water, propping us up. For a time, I believed alongside him, though when we passed under the house's belly in our small fishing boat, I could see that the branches were split and bent, sap-streaked. Our father did not look up, did not seem to worry. When sticky, amber growths burst from the joints of the branches beneath my sister's room, he strung thick ropes between her window frame and the surrounding trees. The ropes held, but the house slowly shifted, dipping the far side closer to the water. Our father added more poles to the sinking half, and whenever they shattered—a sharp sound, like a finger breaking— he disappeared beneath the house to fill the space left behind. Upon returning, with a kind simplicity only he could manage, he assured my sister and I that the house would certainly settle.

My growing concern about the state of things found no purchase—not with my sister, who still wandered the house at fourteen years old like a toddler, blank-faced and unspeaking when we came home in the evenings with our daily catch, and not with our father, who didn't speak about the past or the future, and would smile so painfully when I mentioned the house that I couldn't bring myself to continue. We shared our meals at the end of the day, the three of us together at the downstairs table. My father and I talked only about the things we had seen during our time together out on the swamp. My sister ate slowly and blinked at the window.

It was not a surprise when the kitchen tiles finally went soft in the middle. The kitchen was at the lowest point on the tilted side of the house, and by the time we left in the morning, my wading boots were leaving behind small pits of water wherever I stepped on the first floor, squeezing moisture from the boards. When we returned in the evening, our father avoided the sight for as long as he could, but after dinner, the swamp began to spill in streams through the lowest living room windows, spilling across the floor. I took my sister by the hand and pulled her up the stairs; as always, she did not want to be touched and thrashed in my grip. Our father followed behind us, his face strange and hollow in a way I had never seen before. The water didn't make a sound as it filled the first floor.

This had all happened two days ago.

Tonight, there was blood on the floor for the first time. My sister went ahead of me down the long hallway between our rooms and his. I slid my socked feet a few inches at a time, bracing against the gentle gravity sucking us down the tilted decline. The air around us was warm and smelled of fish—the swamp's scent, intensified by the heat of the night. Beyond the windows, the moon shone through the windows, nearly full.

To my left, over the edge of the railing, malformed armchairs and couches rose from the water on the first floor, swollen with the dark liquid. The water made our house feel bottomless.

My sister was barefoot, her ragged shorts pulled up to mid-thigh and tee shirt hanging loosely from her thin shoulders. As we passed the stairway down to the first floor, she crouched and pressed her hands to the ground to balance herself. She waited, unmoving. In the half-light, her eyes were glossy and black like the eyes of a small dog.

"Go ahead," I said. She was still staring at nothing, still on all fours. I couldn't escape the unease I felt beside her. The lack of speech, lack of expression—our father and I had borne the weight of her strangeness between us without understanding. These nights, it settled on me alone. "Go ahead," I said again.

My sister rose and we began to move. Our father's blood trail tapered off near the hallway's end, where the floor grew steeper, and I reached out for the wall to steady myself. My other hand settled on my sister's shoulder. She made a choked animal sound and stepped away from the touch, out of reach. I felt guilty, and angry for having to feel so.

Our father's bedroom door was just ahead.

"He's inside," I said. It was obvious, but speaking aloud comforted me.

I wanted her to go in instead of me. I had tried to care for him myself, the first night. He had touched every corner of his room, every picture, his gaze slipping from my face without recognition when I grasped his arms. The strangeness in him made me feel unsteady. Surely my sister felt less affected than I did, seeing him like that. I could count on one hand the things which seemed to leave an impression on her.

She put her ear against the door.

"Can you hear anything?" I asked.

She passed her thumb over the red marks near the handle, close beside her cheek. The swiped blood looked black in the low light. He must have hurt himself, but to what extent, I didn't know. There was no pattern to how he behaved. On the second night, he had left his room to sit on the stairway and watch the drowned floor below. I had been too afraid to approach. The feverish flush crept up the back of his neck, and his breath came out in rough, catching bursts.

Tonight, soon after I put my sister to bed, he had wandered into my room holding the large pail we used for bait—worms, night-crawlers, scraps of fish organs. His hunched form approached the side of my bed. He fell to his knees and dragged the lip of the bucket against the grain of the bedroom floor in a violent scooping motion, ripping splinters from the planks. Some phantom urgency made him shake. Moonlight spread from the window behind me across his wiry, sun-spotted shoulders. I called him by name and gripped my sheets in my fist. He was too close, closer than he had been since the first night I approached him in his room. He did not stop, but began to speak.

"Bail it out. Get rid of it—*out.*" He jammed the bucket into the floor with the coiled strength of both arms. "*Out.*"

The words were nonsense, though I could feel my mind struggling to twist them into a shape that I could understand. I saw then that he was bleeding, a gash cut through his cotton tank-top, streaking his stomach. Blood shone on the rim of the pail. My sister stood in the doorway, flat-eyed and staring. For a terrible moment, I felt cornered by the both of them, doubly trapped by their odd behavior.

He stood, face flushed to the neck. He turned, crossed the room, pushed past her and down the sloped hallway, clutching the pail still. She had watched him go without expression.

"Can you hear anything?" I asked my sister again.

The intimacy of the hallway's darkness pressed close around us now that we had stopped moving. The light was dimmer than it had been, back at the top of the stairs. She pulled back from the bedroom door. She was very small, and I knew in part of my mind that it wasn't right for me to force her first into the room. I put my palm on the copper door handle and leaned forward, letting the door drift slowly open; a wedge of deeper darkness yawned wider.

"Go." My voice tightened, and I stepped back to make space, herding her with one hand.

My sister moved into the gap. She looked back. I clenched my insides and shifted my body forward to block the doorway. The angle of the floor pulled me deeper into the room. I braced my forearms against either side of the frame.

"Stay with him. Make sure he doesn't hurt himself any more," I said.

I could hear his body moving in the sheets within the room. The sound was not the slow shift of someone nearly asleep, but a thrashing frenzy, as though he was trying to kick at something or escape. It disturbed me, the energy of it. Our father did not move quickly, not when he was himself.

My sister's eyes jumped to the air above my right shoulder and back to the floorboards, her fingers curling and uncurling.

In a small way, I liked her expression. I liked that I could, for once, guess what she was thinking, as though she wasn't odd, as though we were really the same.

She disappeared into the room. I eased the door handle toward me until the lock clicked into place and I could no longer hear the movements of my father in the bed. I pressed my back to the closed door. The house's tilt tugged my body gently against the wood. I shut my eyes. Sealing the two of them within one room brought me a sense of restored rightness. I imagined her sitting cross-legged on the floor at the foot of his bed, head tipped against the wooden frame, eyes fixed on the wall. She was not afraid, just blank-faced and hardly present, like a stone. My father moved endlessly in the sheets behind her. He could not break free of what he saw, and the more he saw, the more he felt moved to change what was to come. The house was talking to him. The poles were shattering beneath him. The pail was on the pillow beside his, tucked like a second head beneath the sheets.

The more I imagined, the more the sense of rightness husked away. The images were strange, as though it was no longer myself at the root of them. I opened my eyes and stepped away from the door. Fish-smelling heat forced itself down my throat.

The rotten house yawned around me, threatening to close.

***

I woke up with my head already aching. My bedroom was off from its normal alignment in small degrees—the colored glass mobile above my head dangling not-quite straight down. I sat up. Above my headboard, the window had no covering, and sunlight came in through the cypress canopy outside to spread across my lavender sheets. The color was so beautiful and out of place in the darkened room that I felt suddenly sick with loneliness and thought of calling my sister in to look. I swung my legs out of bed. An upraised needle of wood sank halfway through my sock and embedded in the meat of my big toe.

I hissed, tight throat breaking the noise into two parts. I rocked backward onto the bed. Heat spilled up my whole leg with each throb. For a moment, I had forgotten entirely about the night's events, my father's outburst, the shrapnel from the gouged floor.

"You awake? I'm taking the boat out."

It was my father. I pinched my nails together at the base of the splinter, breathing deep through my nose. I could picture him standing at the closed door, weak chin bobbing above his throat. Unaware and beseeching. Spikes of cold nausea shot through me whenever my nails brushed directly against the wood.

"Want to come along?"

I forced out all my air and pulled in one strong movement. My father's simplicity, which had always opposed my sister's strangeness, was contaminated by the shadow of the fevers. The splinter bent as it exited, splitting the skin even further. Blood appeared along the fresh, pink crease, then bloomed outward into the fabric of my sock. I looked away, pressed my forehead to my knees, and whined.

"The weather doesn't seem too bad, today. I expect we'll catch something at that little cove you found."

He paused. My noises carried freely into the emptiness. I wanted him to hear me, and didn't. I knew he didn't have the capacity to comfort me. He had no memory of the night's events, if his behavior on our fishing trips the past two days was true.

"Just… let me know," he said. It was clear that he didn't know what to say. "And don't forget your boots. It's wet below."

Dragging footsteps receded down the hallway. With his absence, I began to cry aloud, cradled in the swath of sunlight. The sight of the tilted furniture around me drove my vertigo deeper than ever, an aching sense of the world being off-balance.

***

Eventually, the sky disappeared, swallowed by the trees. We moved through the water slowly, and my father sat across from me in the boat, one arm draped over the boat's side, the other resting on the motor's heat-melted rubber handle. Our fishing poles lay across my lap, hooks hitched to the stucco grips. The bait pail leaned against my knee. The motor sputtered. My hair hung in a clump over my shoulders, the shorter strands plastered in sweaty curls to my neck and forehead. Heat swelled around us, trapped by the low-hanging branches shadowing our passage.

My father rocked to the right. The front of the boat turned, splitting through the green algae on the swamp's surface, leaving behind a streak of clear, dark water in our wake.

"Mm," he said. He smiled and kept his eyes far ahead, gaze cast over my shoulder. "Maybe. Maybe."

I watched him hollowly, wrists draped between my knees, lips parted. I still felt nauseous from my breakfast. The ice in the salvaged cooler had melted, and the last of our preserved fish inside were warm and sticky to the touch, scales dissolving into white slime. My sister had stepped back at the stench that unfurled when I slid the lid aside. I had reached inside, wrapped a catfish carefully in my hands, and bit into the thickest part. The sour flesh slipped into the back of my throat before I could swallow. I handed my sister the rest.

"It's good," I had told her.

Whatever we caught today wouldn't last. Our father was the one who bought ice for us, made the long trek along the boardwalk back into town. Since the fever, he hadn't been away from the house except to fish with me, and there was no way to cook, as our kitchen stove was underwater, swallowed by the rising swamp.

My mind re-ordered things that way. Rising swamp, not sinking house.

"We'll pull in up here," my father said.

There was a small stretch of very shallow water. He turned off the motor and leaned over the boat's edge, reaching for a nearby branch to push off from. The rip in his wifebeater yawned wider with the movement. Another wave of nausea sent saliva pooling into my mouth.

"Push pole?" he asked. He reached out a hand to me.

I couldn't understand how he was still fine, still moving. He didn't eat anything that my sister brought him, nothing that we caught—she always returned the uneaten fish to me, presenting it. This morning had been the same. Our usual dinner at the downstairs table had become a huddled meeting between my sister and I, alone in my room with the cooler of rotting fish. My father did not leave his room once he returned from fishing, not until the fever came upon him.

I turned and spit my mess into the water. The saliva settled on top of the algae, still within sight.

"You alright?" He asked.

He touched my leg. I moved away, making the bait pail clang against the side of the boat, tin against tin. He watched my reaction stupidly, mouth open like a baby's imitation of surprise. I had avoided his touch without thinking. The combination of his simplicity and ignorance was sour in my chest.

"Did I do something?" he asked.

I stood up and sent the two fishing poles from my lap clattering to the bottom of the boat. A burst of pain flared in my left big toe. I rocked onto it, chasing the feeling. Dragonflies buzzed around my head, wings clicking.

"Let me do it," I said. "You're hurt."

He must have taken my blank expression for pity, because he smiled.

"I'm feeling fine—it's such a small thing." He patted his stomach, fingered the rip in the fabric. "Sleepwalking again. I woke up with the old pail in bed. Must've cut myself somehow."

I latched onto the push pole underneath my seat, and drew it out. The long piece of metal felt good and solid in my hand.

"Let me," I said. My jaw clenched.

"Alright then. Thank you."

I twisted the pole, stretching the segments out to their full length, tightening as I went. The branches scraped against my back. My father peered over the side of the boat. He swirled his fingers in the water to clear the algae and stared into the black spot led behind.

"Strange how little you can see down there," he said.

I pushed the pole down into the swamp beside his head, the movement revealing the water underneath. The tendrils of black spun slowly through the green, reaching outward.

***

I awoke all at once, my lower body already pivoting out of bed and onto the floor. I had managed to fall asleep, but now couldn't make sense of the time of day—the crickets buzzed outside, but pale, blue light came faintly through my window, as though the sun had already risen.

Someone was running in the hallway.

The sound was so out of place in the house, so loud in the darkness, that despite the night's humid swell I felt cold down my entire back. I stood without moving and listened. Heels against wood. Passing closer and then farther. The cadence remained set for some time.

I walked forward, adjusting to the slow, crooked pull of gravity. The footsteps passed far away, and I opened the door, just a small amount. From my new position, I could hear a second sound coming from the floor below. It was the same as I had heard last night when standing in the doorway of my father's room. Splashing.

I stepped out into the hallway and saw that my sister's room was already open across from mine. The sight drew my breath back into my chest, sharp. The hallway stretched out in front of me. I could hear both the splashing and the footsteps clearly now.

"Dad?"

I moved in bursts, one hand feeling along the wall. I wanted to find him, but not her.

"Dad?"

The pounding footsteps came much closer, the vibrations shivering under my feet. The noise seemed impossibly large, expanding into the whole house. I couldn't see well enough to determine who was coming toward me, and the fear grew larger, stopping me and pressing my body against the wall, my arm bent out in front of me. The footsteps stopped.

My arm lowered. It was my sister. She stared at me, her short blond hair clinging to her face. She did not look afraid. Against my wishes, heat sprung to my eyes, threatened to spill. I couldn't believe that she had reduced me to such a state. "Why aren't you asleep?" I rasped.

Her expression remained the same. My desire for a response, an explanation of some sort, curdled in my chest, and I stood to my full height. I grabbed her wrist before she could react, fingers overlapping around the thin bone.

"Come on," I said.

I dragged her to the open section overlooking the first floor, moving with sharp pulls that nearly caused us both to stumble down the slope. From the moment I touched her, she fought against me. She scraped my arm with her nails and twisted her shoulders away. The pain only deepened my satisfaction at her violent reaction. I refused to bear the weight of whatever strangeness lay ahead without her.

The swamp lapped at the staircase leading down below us. My

sister stood behind me, still trying to escape my grip, but the feeling settled into the back of my head like white noise. Ahead, the flooded room was black except for the pale blue light shining through the windows.

Between the silhouettes of half-drowned furniture, our father swam with sloppy strokes. The water was undisturbed except the thrashing movement of him crossing through the room. Each time his arm drew back, his face appeared small and white above the sheet of thick swamp water, gasping for air. He swam from the couch into the kitchen, then beneath us to the front door, then back to the couch. He traced the same path without breaking in pace, eyes fixed on the dark stretch in front of him.

I took a step backward. The fear from before was returning, gathering the longer I watched our father swim. The swamp crept further up the staircase, pushed by our father's passing body, licking over my left sock. It was warm like a mouth. Both of my hands were empty and hung at my sides; I had released my sister's wrist without realizing. My father slipped backward into the water, and my chest ached with pent-up breath, as though the whole house had already been filled.

*- Sierra Myer*

# SEVERANCE

april: to hatch

in the beginning, you walk across the bridge, alone,
toward your first love.the river is hardly speaking,
but it feels the long pull.you hold hands, kiss in the woods,
and summer-comes.  everything in the world is held between.

the windows open wide.
the hardwood floors in a room full of light, faraway, in a house on the hill.


may: subtext

once, inside the voices and the glitter at the celebration luncheon,
as you talked, I watched your left-hand palm-up resting over the green silk
dress in folds across your lap like a boat on the sea.
your right hand lay on the table
mapping the single-creviced edge

of the silver butter knife. almost a caress. rhythmic.
you were a compass pointing north, northeast.


june: water

I dreamed we were salamanders and you said, *I will teach you to float.*
and so, one day, in the middle of the lake, we let the boat drift away.
without touching, you said, *tip your head back. throw your arms out wide;*
*let your hips rise. it feels like a swan dive back, and—* all I can see is blue.

suspended in the sky. held up to the very edge of this liquid earth.
your voice across the water inside me. laughing.

level with the waves. my heart. loved like that.

july: water

the light on your skin breaks into amber, violet, lavender, green.
fractures at the curve of your hip and the shadows drawing in. something
electric there between you and the simple air. we are drying in the sun,
talking, and I say what I see.

that you are made of light. that I am falling in.
a line I can never cross. should never have crossed.


august: deciduous

it came as a map. a survey of lines. a letter. that you read aloud.
a distance written in. a stop.

in this country, drought makes things resinous. longing
is dust hardened with sap. pinon. juniper. sage. you touched my hand.
*it is a map*, you said. my thirst growing like wind.

it feels a kind of fire. a lie. sedimentary. mine.


september: ink

I hadn't noticed before. our letters held their silences.
and though we both entered, alone, together, it was not a place
we could actually go. it was a room in our hearts we had made.
with separate doors.

I watched the yellow warblers come and leave.
I made you presents I could not give, and then the ravens.

I think of you writing your last note in the morning light, the tea
and the honey, the pressed flowers, your reticence. but you spoke
what I could not. *there is no going back.*
and then it was just me.

december: tempest

once, you held your hand to my back, and I could feel the sun,
and I knew that you could never leave. and once,
shoulder to shoulder, I could feel the gravity between us,
and that we were bound together in a way I could not speak.

but I was a swarm of locusts in a blizzard with nowhere to land.
one by one, I fell out of the sky.


may: severance

you asked what I wanted. as if I could say. as if naming
could make it possible. but I cannot.

and you, wiser than me, nod, then smile, then turn,
then walk into the light of the day.


january: paris

otherwise, the sky
would be white as the inside rooms of spring

a wind across the steppe
a silvered roof, bare arms, outstretched.

instead, the rowan tree with her crimson scarves
turns on her heel, whirls away. again.

*- **William S. Barnes***

# ONE HUNDRED THOUSAND STEPS

HE KNOWS THE END IS NEAR when he begins to dream of himself as he is, rather than as he was. No more dreams of bounding through the woods, the trees that flank him acting as spectators who admire his movement and cheer as he passes. No more dreams of running beside his wife in the springtime, listening to her gush over the blooming flowers that line the road while they breathe air heavy with the coming rain. In Larry's dreams now he moves slowly, painfully, always through a fog of fear, always counting. The same way he moves when he is awake.

Larry wasn't alarmed at the initial swelling or the light rash on his left leg. He just assumed it was an allergic reaction. His doctor reassured him that it was probably nothing serious. They tried creams, ointments, antibiotics. When nothing worked, his doctor referred him to an allergist, who, after finding no allergies, was equally confounded. Larry returned to his primary care doctor, who said, Sometimes we see this, an unexplained cellulitis – a skin irritation – and it takes a few months for it to respond to the antibiotics. Then it clears up and we never know the cause. Keep up the antibiotics and let me know how it goes.

Larry took his antibiotics, but he could tell that the rash and the swelling were worsening. The swelling increased markedly after a run, but he pushed through, relying on his years of experience running through discomfort in the military, on all the runs he'd logged while tired or sick. After six weeks of no improvement, he sought out a new general practitioner, Dr. Goodwin. When Larry described how his symptoms hadn't changed over a couple of months, Dr. Goodwin ordered an abdominal ultrasound. Larry asked why, and Dr. Goodwin said, I just want to rule out any arterial issues.

He stares at his white bathroom ceiling, and the tiny shadows cast by the popcorn surfacing remind him of the surface of the moon. Living in a hot climate, he'd organized his summer training schedule around the moon's phases. Though he knew the moon emitted neither, he saw it as a source of both heat and light, an ally against the encroaching darkness and falling temperatures of night. The full moon brought his longest run of the month, and, during the second hour, when the road was flat and straight, he would look upward and feel as though he were running toward it. It was as if fatigue brought with it not only clarity but magnification. And a slight rise in the road would fill him with the euphoric feeling of liftoff.

The ultrasound did not rule anything out. Rather, Dr. Goodwin's voice became quiet as he pointed to a ghostly bulge on the screen. You see this, Mr. Griffin? That's your internal iliac artery. It's difficult to get a clear view on ultrasound. What I see here concerns me, however – I think there is a possibility that what we're seeing is an aneurysm.

Dr. Goodwin told Larry that he needed a CT scan and a consultation with a vascular surgeon. Larry wasn't sure what this meant, but when Dr. Goodwin began to tell him where the vascular surgeon's office was, Larry thought, Right now? Things must be serious.

The office was on another floor and when Larry arrived they directed him down the hall for the CT scan. Larry lay on the concave carbon fiber table and listened to the tech. The X-ray beam will rotate around your midsection and generate a 3D image. Please remain still. It will only take a few minutes. With a thin hum, the table slid forward until the donut-shaped console that had been at his feet encircled his waist. Larry's heart palpitated, as if stimulated by the radiation.

He turns his head and looks back at the faint layer of filth that marks his path from his bed to the bathroom. Filth comprised of the accumulated grime that clings to his skin from not showering in weeks. The electric wheelchair he'd sworn he would not use had stopped working two weeks prior, but he didn't want to call anyone to come fix it, didn't want to see anyone at all. He'd been using it for almost a month, when he had grown frightened of otherwise having only a few days left. He remembers telling Dr. Goodwin, I won't grovel to stay alive. I can at least go out with my dignity intact. The thought of saying those words almost makes him laugh.

Larry thinks about calling Dr. Goodwin, about apologizing for the spiteful, uncomfortable end to their relationship, imagining Dr. Goodwin might tell him that maybe he could be treated after all. There were times when such a thought would have brought him hope and tears. He observes the thought now but feels nothing and resumes his crawl. He cannot imagine a cure, a life of unlimited steps, a life that ends in an unexpected fashion at an unexpected time. The journey to the toilet complete, he pulls himself atop it and then listens to the intermittent tinkle of his urine, trying to envision his insides, where the growing aneurysm presses against his bladder like an unwanted child. He does not think of the aneurysm in the possessive sense, does not consider it his like he does other organs and body parts. He thinks of it as the aneurysm, a foreign invader, an unwelcome intruder, an apocalyptic threat.

Dr. Brennig, the vascular surgeon, told him that it was inoperable. Your extensive internal scarring, particularly between your heart, aorta, and iliac artery, eliminate surgery as an option. Larry's scarring had occurred eight years ago, when he had driven over an improvised explosive device in Afghanistan. He remembered none of it, though Jamey, a laid-back private from Oklahoma City who visited him in the hospital stateside, had told him, Dude, you were fileted open like a mackerel.

Jamey's words were in Larry's mind as he tried to picture himself immediately after the explosion, which is what he was doing while Dr. Brennig was talking. There was mostly blankness there, and, while he always told people he was thankful that he didn't remember, the truth was he ached to fill that gap. He felt like, if he could only remember, then things would somehow be better. But the few memories of that day were faint as scents, and his mind wandered between them like a dog off leash, investigating the mysterious and reveling in the familiar, lingering indiscriminately.

He pulled himself away from the past and tried to attend to Dr. Brennig. Sorry. I'm struggling to absorb all this. You can't fix it. Okay. So what's next? Is there some drug? Or do these ever just go away?

Well, as for what's next, Mr. Griffin. I think you'd be best off discussing that with Dr. Goodwin. He can present you with some options as far as hospice care and pain management. As for medication or whether this could resolve itself... Well. I'm not aware of any aneurysms like yours that did not eventually rupture if left untreated. However, there are some medications we can prescribe to reduce the risk of a clot breaking free and causing an embolism. We can also prescribe blood pressure meds. Lower blood pressure will put less stress on the vessel. That at least could buy you some additional time.

How much time do I have? Larry asked, feeling like he was reading a script in a bad movie.

Dr. Brennig smiled. And, though his round face and white hair and wire-rimmed glasses gave him a sort of grandfatherly benevolence, the smile did not convey warmth. Unfortunately, I can't really answer that at this point. Your aneurysm is about nine centimeters. A recent study found internal iliac aneurysms ranging from two centimeters to thirteen centimeters at the time of diagnosis, and, while the point of rupture was similar, sometimes those that were smaller initially progressed faster. It really is unpredictable until we've monitored its growth for a period.

He crawls back toward his bed as his leg pulses, a clock that cannot be rewound marking off its final ticks. Though he has stopped going to the doctor, he has continued charting his steps and knows he has less than five thousand. He is thin now, and his body feels heavy and firmly rooted to the ground. Some days he sits in a chair by his front window and watches life in his neighborhood continue. The elderly on their walks, the mothers pushing strollers, the joggers – all of them seem alien to Larry. Their movement is so free and light, as if gravity affects them differently. Larry realizes that he has become a spectator, that the world in which he used to be a participant is little more than a backdrop now, and he can step into it about as easily as he can step into his television screen. He wonders if this is a common feeling for the old and decrepit, and he weeps, thinking, But I'm only thirty-five.

Larry was skeptical when Dr. Goodwin told him he had around 100,000 steps left. It took a half dozen visits to arrive at the number. When Dr. Goodwin first said it, Larry rose from the exam table and took two steps forward. Uh-oh, Doc. 99,998 now.

Dr. Goodwin didn't smile. He just pointed again to the CT scans and the graph that plotted his steps against the growth of the aneurysm.

Larry, I know it is hard to believe, but look at this. We can accurately measure the rate of growth of your aneurysm between each of your last six visits. We can compare the growth to the amount of time elapsed and, since you've been wearing the pedometer, we can also compare it to the number of steps you took between each visit, okay?

Larry nodded.

It appears that your aneurysm is worsening with each step. I discussed why that might be with Dr. Brennig, and we think that, because of your internal scarring, the movement of your leg pulls on the aneurysm in such a way that causes more rapid expansion. Look at how much less it worsened during the 48 hours you spent in bed.

Dr. Goodwin had assigned Larry to bed rest between two of the visits, and the CT scan taken at each showed the aneurysm did grow more slowly during that period.

Alright, Dr. Goodwin. So what I am supposed to do? Stay in bed until I keel over?

No, Larry, that's not what I'm advocating. I'm just encouraging you to think about how you use your steps. We know about at what point these aneurysms will rupture, and, projecting the rate of growth we saw during your bed rest period… Well, I'd guess you could increase your time left by more than tenfold if you utilize a wheelchair. It will still rupture eventually, but you can delay it.

Larry ignored the suggestion of the wheelchair and focused on the 100,000 steps.

So 100,000 steps. I've been using, what, 4,000 a day? So you're saying that in 25 days this thing'll rupture and that'll be it. A month. Am I wrong?

Dr. Goodwin bent forward, the wheeled stool beneath him squeaking as he moved. Not 25 days, Larry. 100,000 steps. Sure, if you take 4,000 steps a day you'll have around twenty-five days. But if you use a wheelchair, you'll probably live another year. Dr. Goodwin leaned back and folded his hands in his lap, as if he had delivered satisfactory news.

One week later, Larry walked into Dr. Goodwin's office wet with sweat, for he had gone for a run. He had been angry, knowing that Dr. Goodwin would be pushing a wheelchair on him later that day. He thought running would prove something. He'd taken off his pedometer and, for a few steps, he felt like he'd traveled back in time. But as his heart rate climbed, a sense of building pressure rose up his thigh and into his belly. The pressure welled up with each contact with the pavement, and he couldn't help but count. And so, after less than three miles, 5,000 steps, just two laps around his neighborhood, he stopped, knelt on the pavement, and sobbed.

Dr. Goodwin greeted him warmly but became grave as he examined the new CT scan.

Have you been wearing your pedometer? The aneurysm is expanding faster than I would have projected, given the number of steps you recorded.

Larry could see no reason to lie. Doc, I went for a run.

Dr. Goodwin tilted his head and squinted, as if he were confused. You ran? How far? You must not have worn your pedometer. Dr. Goodwin spoke the last sentence as though he were reassured that his calculations weren't incorrect, that it was a matter of patient noncompliance.

Larry cut him off before he could say anything else. Look, I needed to run. I mean, this whole thing seems like science fiction. Or it did. But I could feel something on that run, a lot worse than my run from six weeks ago, a lot worse than it feels when I'm walking.

How long was the run?

Maybe three miles. And yeah, I counted. Around five thousand steps.

Dr. Goodwin jotted something on his pad.

Larry, based on how the aneurysm looks today, I'd guess that each running step actually costs you a bit more than walking. I'd say that each running step is worth about one and a half walking steps. So a 5,000-step run is equivalent to roughly 7,500 steps walking.

Larry nodded and said nothing.

Is it really worth it? Doctor Goodwin asked.

Well, I love running, Larry said. Maybe that's silly, but it's true.

Doctor Goodwin frowned for a moment, then smiled. Surely you love other things as well, though, Larry. Things that aren't so costly to your health. Family? Friends? Don't you think they'd appreciate you sticking around a little longer?

Larry was quiet, thinking, If I'm not going to pursue a love just because the price is high, what does that say about love? And then he thought about his departed parents, his estranged sister, and his ex-wife. No, Dr. Goodwin, I don't have a lot of strong social ties. I'm divorced and my parents passed a few years ago… And I've thought about the wheelchair thing. I don't want one. I don't want to die in a chair. If someone told you that you could live an extra twenty years but that you'd have to live in a chair for the rest of your life to do it, would you?

Well, Larry, no one has presented me with that option. I do see your point, however. How about I order the chair, and you can try it out? No one will make you sit in it. If you're concerned about the cost, I'm confident we can establish a service connection, in which case the VA will cover it.

Larry wanted to tell Dr. Goodwin his mind wasn't really on cost since he only had a month to live. He wanted to tell the doctor to fuck off, to stop trying to force him into a chair. But he didn't want things to end badly. He liked Dr. Goodwin.

Okay. Order the chair. I'm not saying I'll use it, though. Also, I was thinking, if I only have a certain number of steps left, I think I'll end my visits to your office. No offense, but I don't know if it's worth a few hundred steps every week if there's no treatment for me.

Dr. Goodwin seemed surprised. That's your decision, Larry. I am concerned, though, because we won't be able to monitor the aneurysm from afar. It might advance slower or faster than we expect. When Larry didn't respond, Dr. Goodwin continued, seeming mildly perturbed that Larry would choose to go unmonitored. But if that's what you want, that's fine. How about I make a house call to check on you in a few weeks? Dr. Goodwin looked at him as though he should be grateful for this offer.

Larry stared back, wondering why the man couldn't understand that knowing when the end would come was not purely a blessing. Being able to quantify the percent of his life he expended while walking from his bedroom to his kitchen did not feel like something to be thankful for. He thought such knowledge might cause him to go mad before he died. But he decided to agree, reluctantly, though there was one more thing he wanted to know.

He lowered his head, looking at his feet, noticing his running shoes, and thinking himself absurd and pathetic. Then he asked, What'll it feel like?

Pardon me?

What'll it feel like, Doc? You know, at the end.

Dr. Goodwin tried to dodge the question at first, telling Larry maybe that wasn't the best thing to focus on. But Larry insisted. Finally, Dr. Goodwin told him he would probably feel a tearing, a sudden flash of pain followed by lightheadedness. Then, he said, you'll probably pass out. He didn't say that Larry would not wake up.

It is sometime after one in the morning, and the bathroom floor is cold. Larry tried to keep his nighttime trips to the toilet to a minimum, but he'd drunk three beers around ten o'clock. The transition from warm bed to cold tile jars him to alertness. From his position on the floor, he cannot see the moon, though its pale light casts shadows through his bathroom window. He remembers that it is full, and he suddenly has the urge to feel its light shine directly on him, and his breathing becomes shallower and more rapid with excitement. He reaches up and grips the sink, pulling himself to his knees. Then he plants his right foot in front of him, places both hands on his thigh and presses up as he stands, slowly, mechanically, frame by frame. A pop emanates from his right kneecap, unused to bearing his weight. He wavers, distracted by the phantasmal image in the mirror. He hasn't looked in a mirror in over a month, since before Dr. Goodwin made his house call. He can't recall how long it has been since he last saw himself in the moonlight. The light is not adequate for him to see his own eyes, and he is frightened by his face, by his eye sockets hollow and dark. A breeze outside waves a tree limb in front of the moon. The movement of the shadows disorients him, and he thinks for a moment that he will fall. Then he steadies himself and looks outside, where the world seems bright as day.

The house call only happened once, and it was two weeks after his last appointment. It didn't go well. He answered the door on his feet, and Dr. Goodwin almost immediately admonished him for not using the wheelchair. Then he tried to persuade Larry that he should try meditation or maybe counseling. Larry remembered his ex-wife telling him that he should meditate a year or so after he'd returned from Afghanistan. He had tried it a couple times, but his meditations were filled with trauma, not peacefulness. He didn't tell Dr. Goodwin that, though. Instead, he said, Thanks, Doc. But I don't have the patience for meditating and I don't have the time for counseling. I've got to conserve steps, remember?

Dr. Goodwin nodded and said that he wanted to talk to him about that. Then he tried to convince Larry to move into a clinic or an assisted living facility where he would be more comfortable and, who knew, maybe a new surgical technique would come out and give him a shot at a cure.

Larry said it was out of the question, that this was his home, and he had memories here to accompany him to the end. He wasn't leaving. He accused Doctor Goodwin of only wanting to help him so that he could publish some sort of case study or capitalize on him in some way. He had no idea as to whether that was true, he'd only heard Dr. Brennig talk about the rarity of these types of aneurysms and how few relevant case studies there were in the literature.

Dr. Goodwin avoided the confrontation and left, wishing Larry good luck and telling him to let him know if he had further questions about his condition.

Larry did not speak to him again. He did begin to doubt Dr. Goodwin and Dr. Brennig, however, so he requested his medical records and sent them on to two other vascular surgeons with a request for an opinion, explaining in a written note why he didn't come in person. The other two surgeons gave him the same response: there was nothing they could do for him.

By the time Larry shuffles outside, the moon seems to have reached its peak in the sky. His neighborhood street is empty and bright, the street lamps rendered unnecessary by the moon. He steps down from his porch onto the sidewalk, and his leg quivers, weak and unsteady. He is barefoot, and the pavement feels rough under his feet. One foot moves forward and then another, and, though his street is flat, he feels like he is moving downhill, an unseen force pulling him forward, his legs just barely keeping up. Momentum accumulates and soon he is airborne for that split second between the striking of the ball of each foot. The mailboxes and the houses seem strange, otherworldly, and watching them rush by nauseates him. He turns his gaze to the ground, thinking about how it feels under his feet and not about how soon he will be beneath it. He zigs and zags back and forth across the street, running up into lawns, feeling the blades of grass buckling beneath him. Clouds move across the moon, and Larry has the illusion that they are stationary and that he is moving across the landscape so rapidly it changes their relative position. Then he is on the ground.

Another explosion, Larry thinks, as the blood rushes out from his burst vessel into his body cavity. The sensation is not as painful as he had feared. He is in the middle of the street and the asphalt around him mirrors the sky, dark and uniform, any stars or irregularities drowned out by the moonlight. His blood, which once ran so precisely through his veins and arteries and vessels, begins to pool beneath him, a layer of warm liquid just beneath the skin. Yet he grows colder, and he thinks that perhaps he was wrong about the moon, that perhaps the moon is actually a hole in the night's fabric, a point of ventilation through which the day's heat escapes. He tries to imagine a sky of whiteness as bright as the moon, covered by a shroud, and he thinks, That would be a white light, after all. Then he tries to picture what a world beneath such a sky would look like, and the moon seems to move, and he thinks he can feel its gravity. Finally, his body lies still on the asphalt, all the blood inside him unloosed, free to wash back and forth like the tide.

*- Victor McConnell*

# Vickmeyer Falls

VICKMEYER FUNCTIONED LIKE CLOCKWORK.

He came out on his side stoop every morning at 7:30 sharp. In the summer he sipped orange juice from a highball glass. The OJ gave way to coffee in a cobalt blue mug in the winter. It had to be coffee. One look at Vickmeyer, and you knew he was a coffee man.

It was dead winter now, mid-February, and I watched from the couch through our picture window as Vickmeyer emerged, mug in hand. He took a sip and exhaled, the steam from his breath twisting into the frigid air.

I kept watching. The only sound in our house came from upstairs as my wife got ready for work.

Vickmeyer looked down. I couldn't tell at what. His lower half was obscured by his 42-inch-high boxwoods. I knew they were 42 inches. They had to be. Vickmeyer told me. He was the Neighborhood Association Regulations Compliance Officer. The acronym was NARCO, but he called himself, understandably, the ARCO.

That's how he had introduced himself to me two summers ago as I sat on my front porch, taking in the new neighborhood. He'd walked up my sidewalk and given me a nod. I asked him if he was the welcome wagon. He just looked at me, then proceeded to nail me on my viburnum shrubs. They were 50 inches. Regulations allowed for a maximum of 42 inches. I told him I'd take care of it. Vickmeyer gave me a look like he didn't believe me. Vickmeyer had good instincts.

I told my wife about the visit.

"They could fine us," she warned.

"For shrubs?" I asked. "Not a chance."

They fined us two days later.

Vickmeyer took another sip of his coffee, turned and went into his house. Another minute passed. He reemerged with a plastic cup. It was salt. He moved down one step, flicking away. And then he vanished. Maybe not vanished. I saw his arms twirl back, the plastic cup fly, a flash of his kicking legs. And then he vanished. I peered through my window and waited. Nothing.

"What's so funny?"

It was my wife, coming down the stairs, dressed for work.

"What?" I asked.

"I heard a Ha," she said. "What were you laughing at?"

"Wasn't a laugh," I said. "I sneezed."

Nimble alibis are a natural product of a healthy marriage.

"In that case, gesundheit," she said before kissing me.

My wife moved into the kitchen. I kept watching the space where Vickmeyer had been. I could see vertical wisps of steam rising in steady increments from behind the boxwoods. I waited for him to reemerge, aggravated and embarrassed. But there was no Vickmeyer. Just the rising steam. I stayed on the couch. My wife came back with her travel mug.

"You sending out resumes today?" she asked.

I got that question every Monday. It's how I kept track of time. I had to send out three resumes per week to keep the unemployment checks coming. I picked out three companies from random on the Web. It didn't matter which. They all said the same thing.

"I was thinking," she said as she put on her coat. "Maybe we should change it up. Go somewhere."

"Where?"

"You know, a weekend trip, when the weather gets better."

I didn't answer. She stopped at the door.

"Can you think of a good weekend place?" she asked.

"Sure," I said, trying not to smile. "How about Vickmeyer Falls."

"Vickmeyer as in our neighbor Vickmeyer?"

"Yep."

"Never heard of it. Where's it located?"

"Not far," I said. "I hear it's beautiful."

"Vickmeyer Falls," she said, opening the door. "I'll Google it later."

I watched as she walked to the drive and her car, my eyes periodically shifting over to Vickmeyer's side stoop. He was still down there. I could see the steam rising. My wife didn't. She got in her beige Toyota and pulled away.

My cell phone was on the coffee table. I reached for it and

searched for how long it takes to freeze to death in 26-degree weather. There were too many variables to make a solid estimate, but once Vickmeyer's temperature hit 95 degrees, he was in for some trouble.

The site listed several symptoms for hypothermia. Shivering. Confusion. I thought of one more: no longer caring about your neighbor's viburnums. I let out another Ha. It sounded strange in the empty house.

I was doing a mental coin-toss on whether to call 911 when Daryl's front door opened and he walked out onto his front porch. He lived next to Vickmeyer, but on the opposite side of Vickmeyer's side stoop. He took out a pack of cigarettes from his shirt pocket and lit up. Daryl had come over to introduce himself one day after Vickmeyer's maiden visit. We had something in common. We managed to get laid off in the same week.

Daryl took a long drag and exhaled. He watched the white smoke twist and disappear, then looked over in my general direction. I waved, but I knew he couldn't see me.

I looked back at Vickmeyer's spot. There was still steam coming up, but it seemed less frequent. My phone pinged. It was a text from my wife. She worked just 10 minutes away, and was already at the office.

Googled Vickmeyer Falls. couldn't find it?

I thumbed out a quick reply.

it's so close, practically in our front yard

I let out another Ha. It sounded more natural this time. My phone pinged again.

hm. can't seem to find

keep looking, I replied.

Daryl ground out his cigarette and went back in. I looked over at Vickmeyer's side stoop. There was the faintest sign of steam. I'd put my phone back on the coffee table. I kept looking at it. I had a decision to make. It made me feel relevant for the first time in months. A car passed on the road. I reached for the phone, but my hand stopped midway. It was like it belonged to someone else.

I'd wait for another minute, and then try reaching again.

*- Steven Fromm*

# Abigail

*1 Samuel 35*

I thought Nabal's death a godsend.
Cruel, a drunkard.
Rich yes, but miserly.

David seemed so noble,
so reasonable.
He stayed his anger
when I stepped between.

A man after God's own heart,
so it is said.
Had I not known of Bathsheba,
I might have believed it.
He moons after her
like a calf for its mother.

I shed a miserable husband
for an adulterous one.
Whose heart does he really seek:

God's or the woman he saw
bathing in the moonlight?

*- Charles Darnell*

# JUDITH'S HANDMAID

Book of Judith

You read it in the stories,
seen the paintings.
The great book does not name me,
but I had a hand in it too.
Judith sawed with the sword,
I held him by his greasy hair.

His blood spurted with the first cut,
sprayed my face as she sliced,
no voice to cry out, his eyes bulged
with each blood-pulse
and so, he died.

The people gained heart
and rushed out to defeat the Philistines
exclaiming *Judith!*
She was carried high on shoulders
of the joyous people,

But I,
I carried Holofrenes' head.

- Charles Darnell

# An Investment

I STOOD UNDER THE CANOPY of the hotel's entrance, my back to the sea, facing the only road to the beach. The mountains were a purple haze in the distance.

The place was deserted, the last of the summer stragglers long gone and the bite of winter already in the air. I rubbed my hands and shifted from foot to foot to keep warm. Besides my rental, there were only two vehicles in the car park. I saw him approach the hotel from a long way out. The car looked ancient – a black Volkswagen with patches of grey where the rust had been removed and painted over with a primer. And patches of brown where new rust was showing. The back window was plastered with travel stickers from all across Europe. He rolled down the passenger window.

"Hello, stranger." He grinned, exposing his yellow teeth.

"Jesus, you look shit," I said.

"Fuck you," he answered, getting out of the car and coming around to hug me. There was little of him to hug, just skin and bone. He wore jeans, black ankle boots, a grey hoodie and a navy fleece gilet. None too clean. He smelt damp and mouldy.

"You look like a capitalist bastard," he said.

Now, face-to-face with him, I felt overdressed in my fancy outdoor jacket. I was too groomed and manicured.

"I'll bring you into town for a bite," he said, "and then we'll head to my place. Ursula would love to see you."

"Sounds like a plan. How is she?"

"Yeah, grand. You'll see for yourself." He opened the passenger door for me and ran around to the driver's side.

The car was filthy, the ashtray overflowing with butts. There were sweet wrappers and plastic bottles on the floor. The passenger seat was stained and looked sticky. A dirty, grey throw covered the back seat and gave off a whiff of dog. I tried to hide my squeamishness as I sat into the seat.

We drove into a low sun. He leaned forward as he drove, forcing the gear shift into position. "The clutch is on the way out," he said, "like myself."

We settled into the drive. The car rattled and clanked as we made our way.

"I didn't think you'd come."

"Well, here I am."

"Yeah. Here you fucking are. It's brilliant." He looked across at me and grinned the boyish grin that I remembered.

"How did you end up here?"

"Ursula's family had a place and they gave it to her."

"You jammy bastard."

"Yeah."

The road was narrow and twisty, and I shut up to let him concentrate on driving. In the confines of the car, my nerves were grated by his twitching and sniffling.

"And how is Claire," he said, his eyes fixed on the road.

"She's good. Keeps the ship afloat. She knows all about you."

"Really?"

"I played the old songs for her."

"Cool. Ursula reads all about her in the papers."

"Well, don't believe any of the shit they print in the papers."

*

We pulled into the diamond. After the weekend, the town was sleepy. Bobbie led the way, not bothering to lock the car.

"Is The Oak OK?" he asked, as if I knew my way around these parts.

"Whatever you think. You're the man with the knowledge."

The pub was dark inside, old-fashioned. There were two old timers at the bar and the owner was behind the counter. He greeted Bobbie in a booming voice. We sat at a table near the only window.

"What will you have?"

"Is this a lunch stop?" I asked.

"I'm sure Michael will rustle up a toasted special."

"Grand so. And a coffee."

Bobbie grinned. "Good man, Donal. Glad to see you've kept

up your saintly habits."

He came back with a double whiskey for himself.

"Are you not eating?"

"I'll have something later."

I refrained from commenting on the double whiskey at this hour of the day, or the drive to follow. Inwardly, I sighed. And I felt myself tightening. I knew what was coming. I sensed the desperation that had caused him to contact me, after such a long time. I didn't want to despise him but feared I might. He raised his glass. "Sláinte," he said and took a mouthful of the whiskey.

As we waited for the sandwich, he chattered. How he was clean, though cocaine had nearly destroyed him. How amazingly clear his mind was, now the drugs were out of his system. How much more he understood about how the world works. Did I know the moon landing was staged? Was I aware that governments fool us all the time? He seemed intense about his conspiracies, the muscles on his neck taut and vibrating as he spoke. He interrupted his monologue to roll a cigarette and nip outside for a quick smoke.

"I'm writing again," he said, when he came back in, "good stuff, too – enough for an album."

"That's great," I said. "The songs on that first CD have stood the test of time, my friend."

"They weren't half-bad."

And then Bobbie fell into a kind of reverie or a vacancy.

"Have you lived a good life, Donal?"

I laughed. The owner arrived with my sandwich and a mug of coffee before I could answer.

I separated the two slices of bread and let the steam escape. The cheese looked like melted wax. I cut the sandwich into quarters.

"Take one," I said.

"Jesus, couldn't look at it. Too early for me." he said.

I took a bite. It tasted delicious, as only a toasted special, with onion, tomatoes, ham and cheese can taste.

"Well," he insisted. "Have you?"

"I've done all right," I answered, riled at the idea of having to answer to Bobbie, given the fucking state of him.

"I can see that." He grinned, his yellow teeth like those of a wolf. "I fucked up, big time. But you know that. We could have had a half-decent life, Ursula and me. Only I was always running after the next big thing, until I fucking ran out of road." He laughed. "I had none of your steadiness."

"Well, that's one word for it," I said.

"Well, whatever the fuck it is, it served you well, Donal, old pal. Look at you now. A Fat Cat Capitalist Cunt." He looked at me, avidly, his Adam's apple prominent in his scrawny neck. "But I'd never let a few million come between old friends, isn't that right."

"That's right," I said as I mentally checked out of the conversation, and the situation and all the bullshit that went with it. And, in my mind, I was in the rental car heading to the airport.
Bobbie looked around the pub and waved a greeting to the two old timers.

"Do you remember Quinn's in Camden?"

"Of course. Summer of '76."

"Best summer of my life."

"Yeah, right."

"No. I'm serious."

I wasn't going down that rabbit hole. The good old days, the what-might-have-beens. For fuck's sake.

But there was no stopping Bobbie. He called for another whiskey. And then he was off, recalling everything in glorious technicolour. He'd dropped out of college after Christmas and headed off for a few months with a folk/rock band that was the next big thing for a couple of years. After the tour he got a residency in a pub in Camden, moved into a squat, took up with Ursula, who was singing with different groups and working behind the bar in Quinn's. By the time I arrived over after my exams, Bobbie was set up and well on his way to becoming a stoner. I got a job with the council, and the three of us played some gigs together. I could hold a tune and play a few chords, but I had no pretensions or ambitions.

Ursula was few years older than us, with a degree from art school in her back pocket and an ironic disdain for me. She teased me unceasingly; mocked my mammy's-boy morality; my scruples about squatting in someone else's property; my modesty; my caution; my reluctance to experiment; to let go; to be free. "And how's the frightened mouse, today," she'd say. I affected indifference, but she saw through me and enjoyed the alarm she caused me to feel. She'd walk in on me in the bathroom and stay longer than she needed to, looking me up and down. She moaned and groaned theatrically when she and Bobbie had sex. She lit joints for me and teased me into smoking them. I was never comfortable around her and thought I hated her. And wanted her beyond reason. She haunted my dreams.

By the end of summer, I was glad to be going back to college, exhausted by Bobbie's endless plans and notions and the pure shite he talked when he was stoned. And exhausted by my own desires and cowardice. I finished my degree and soon lost interest in following Bobbie's comings and goings, the small successes and bigger setbacks. And I didn't miss him in my life. Occasionally, out of the blue, I'd remember sitting at the counter in Quinn's having a pint that Ursula had pulled, with Bobbie singing in the background, and I lingered in the memory. But that happened less and less and when it did, the memory had lost its power to move me.

***

And then I met Claire at a party in Dublin. I liked her. Liked her calm, her quiet determination, her ease with her family's wealth. After we married, I went into the business full time. We bought failing pubs and restaurants and turned them around. I surprised myself. I had an eye for a deal. I could smell the weakness in those whose businesses we acquired. I enjoyed crushing them.

***

Bobbie would have stayed in The Oak all day.

"I'm sure Ursula will be wondering if I'm trying to avoid her," I said. I offered to drive, but he held his hands up. "Steady as a rock. See." The house was a few miles out of town, into the hills. On the drive he brought up the question of money. Fifteen thousand is what he needed to book a proper studio, with a serious producer and session musicians to record his album, have a launch and do some proper promotion. Fifteen grand. He wouldn't ask only there was no one else he knew who would consider investing in him. Or had the means. But we went back. I knew the real him. This was his shot at redemption. I swear his voice trembled with emotion, with his want.

"And will I get a return on the investment," I said, with a coldness that I reserved for deal-making.

"Well," he laughed, nervously, "maybe not a monetary one."

"Is there another kind?"

"Are you playing me, Donal, you fucker?"

And I laughed, too.

***

Ursula's house sat gable-end to the road, up a rough lane. It was a single-storied farmhouse, plain and sturdy, with a gather of outbuildings behind it. The outside had an air of neglect about it, but nothing irrevocable; nothing beyond the point of no return. We parked the car to the rear. From a shed, a black dog emerged, growling and none too friendly. I was relieved when the chain that secured him tightened and stopped his progress.

"That's Ben," Bobbie said, by way of explanation, "Ursula's dog." He led me in a back door. The narrow hallway opened into a kitchen-cum-sitting room.

I was surprised by how bright and cosy it was, how full of optimism and care, belying the rough track and the exterior. Ursula was sitting by the range. She looked older than I expected and skinny in an unhealthy way. Her face was strained. She wore a white blouse and a long, green gypsy skirt. One leg was resting on a footstool.

"Phlebitis," she answered to the question I hadn't asked. "It's not great today. But I've taken the drugs and once they kick in, I'll be sorted."

I nodded sympathetically.

"You look well," she said, "if a bit over-fed."

"And good to see you too," I answered.

"Sit here by me," she said, laughing at me for taking offence. She gestured to the chair beside her. She lifted her skirt gingerly and showed me her leg.

"Jesus, mercy," I said, at the sight of the ulcerated patches and the discoloured skin.

"I'm waiting for an appointment," she said, and all she didn't say lay between us – the question of money; Bobbie's wants over her needs.

She sent Bobbie off to split some logs and fill the wicker basket she kept by the stove, and watched in her wry way as I surveyed the room, noting the books, and the art on the walls; the absence of any trace of Bobbie's music – no keyboard; no guitars, no fiddle.

"Are they yours," I asked, indicating the paintings.

"Do you like them?"

"They're amazing," I said, with real admiration. They were landscapes inspired by the countryside around, but with startling perspectives and bold dashes of colour, and a light not common this far north. "Do you exhibit?"

"I sell a few through a gallery."

"I can see why they sell. You might sell me one."

"I might, if you're lucky."

"I'd be lucky to have one. Are you still singing?"

"Nah, I gave up on music."

And then it was my turn to study her. The mocking light was still there in her eyes, despite the crow's feet and blemished skin, as was the regal way she had of holding herself, her abundant hair, now silver, piled high on her head like a magnificent crown.

She raised her face. "Well, what's the verdict? Have I survived the wreckage?" Her old self was there in her tone and her look.

"More than survived."

She shook her head and laughed.

"Thank you, Donal. Ever the gentleman."

I gave a mock bow.

"Tell me, do you regret the life you didn't live?" she asked.

"What the fuck," I said. "Did you rehearse this with Bobbie?"

"What?"

"The questions about the life I've led or didn't lead."

"I don't understand?"

"Really? He asked me much the same thing."

"Did he? Well, I'd say he was asking it of himself so. Anyway, tell me now that you've had a practice run, do you regret the life you didn't live?"

As if there was an alternative life to be led. As if a better life was available. I shook my head at the idea. "No, Ursula," I said with deliberation, "I don't regret the life I didn't lead. I appreciate the one I did."

"And very correct, too," she said with mock solemnity.

"What about you," I challenged her, as my eyes swept the room and the world she'd created.

"Me? No way. I'm a Buddhist," she said, laughing. "Didn't you know? I live in the now and practice mindfulness."

"Really?" I scoffed. "Are you mindful of your pain and discomfort?" I said, nodding at her leg.

"Touché. The little mouse has acquired claws."

"They were always there. I just retract them less these days."

Bobbie came back, the basket full to overflowing.

"It's fucking freezing out there," he said, as he filled the stove with logs.

"Come, eat of this feast I've prepared," Ursula said. The table was set with china cups and plates. There was a spread of meats and cheese, relishes and breads. She stood up with the aid of a stick and got Bobbie to place the footstool for her. "You sit there," she said to me, pointing to a chair, "on my good side, away from my bad leg."

We sat side by side, and Bobbie sat opposite me.

There was a lot of passing of plates back and forth, and Bobbie took some meat and bread. The formality of the table, so carefully set with the good china, had an inhibiting effect. I was reminded of those occasions from my childhood when my mother's sisters and their husbands would arrive from the country in their Sunday best and sit at the table in the good room, self-conscious and restricted, as if the occasion robbed them of their own personalities. And everyone praised every aspect of the meal and my mother pressed extra servings on the men, and they accepted, glad to have something to do with their hands and mouths until the agony of the meal passed and they could escape to the back garden for a cigarette, loosen their ties and relax into being themselves.

"So," Ursula said, after we had got through eating, "did Bobbie put his proposal to you?"

"He did," I replied, relaxing into my chair.

"And?"

"I'll consider it."

"You mean, you'll get Claire's approval," Ursula said, smiling.

"Well, I'll certainly consult with her, if that's what you mean. Claire's the brains of the outfit."

"I'd say Claire is a sweetheart," Ursula said, as she threw her head back and laughed. And then her tongue brushed leisurely over her lower lip, in a way I remembered from our days in the squat. And I remembered the wonder of that same tongue as it moved here and there, searching out every corner of my astonished mouth; how it rolled deliciously and pushed against the hard palate before flicking in and out in a rapid succession of teasing darts while I bit down hard on its thickness trying to hold it still. And the way she dismissed me then, pushed me from her, while Bobbie looked on smiling in his doped-up way. Like he looked on now, expectant, hopeful. And how I had done nothing but taken myself away from danger, like a good little boy.

After the dishes were cleared, Bobbie asked if I'd like to hear some of the new music.

"Love to," I said, and I felt Ursula's thigh press against mine as she smiled at me.

"How is your business empire," she asked as Bobbie went off to get his guitar and ready himself to play for us.

"Hardly an empire."

"I read about Claire and you in the papers and the magazines."

"So I heard."

She looked at me with a mocking air. But I held her gaze, and she knew I was now her equal and that amused her, as it did me. And she brushed her good leg against mine again and rubbed her hand on my thigh, slowly and deliberately, and I pushed against her and explored her leg through the thin material of her skirt, and let my fingers sink into the soft flesh of her inner thigh.

Bobbie came back into room. He put some sheets on the table and used a chair as footrest. He played eight of his new songs. Two of them were decent. And his voice had deepened and sounded lived in. The whole thing wasn't half-bad. If the album were produced it would get a few plays on the radio and receive good reviews from the older reviewers. And Bobbie would get invitations to play at some festivals. And he'd feel energised. And then what? Nothing. Bobbie and the album and the fifteen grand would sink without trace. Back in the day, I thought Bobbie was amazing. Now I understood he was never as good as he believed himself to be, and never good enough.

Ursula listened to him and encouraged him like a mother would her child. I saw the forbearance in her attitude but other things, too, like tiredness and loyalty and knowledge. She knew this was a mirage, an older man's folly. I didn't understand the dynamic between them, didn't understand why she was still here with him.

"Well," Bobbie asked when he'd finished.

"You still have it in spades, Bob."

"So what do you think, Mr Investor?"

"I'll think about it and get back to you."

"Sure, what the fuck is there to think about?" And his tone fell somewhere between pleading and petulance.

The drugs, whatever they were, had kept Ursula going all evening, but when they began to wear off, she looked exhausted and with a peck on the cheek took her leave of me and headed to bed. Bobbie checked in after a little while and said she was sleeping.

"Your visit gave Ursula a real lift," he said, "I haven't seen her in such good form in ages. You always managed to spark something in her. Fair play, Donal."

"That's good," was as much as I ventured in return.
Bobbie fetched another guitar, an old Fender steel-string. My fingertips were soft when I went to play a few chords, my joints stiff. Still, I managed to play along as Bobbie rattled through a couple of songs we used to sing together. And then he produced two glasses and a bottle of whiskey. We sipped and played for an hour or more and lost ourselves

in the music, as if it meant something to be old friends singing and playing together. And I suppose it did.

***

It was late when I left, and cold, the stars bright in a high sky. And my breath formed clouds of mist as I moved towards Bobbie's car. The dog stirred and rattled his chain and gave off a few barks and a low growl before settling down. As we drove the dark roads, trees and bushes loomed up in the headlights and threw grotesque shadows round every bend. We said little enough on the journey to the hotel. He pulled up in front of the entrance, the engine idling.

"Thanks for coming," he said. "It means a lot to me, you old bollix."

"I'll be in touch," I answered. I didn't hug him, but I banged the roof of the car before I hurried into the hotel.

In the morning, driving to the airport, I felt benign towards Bobbie. But it was Ursula who was on my mind, the way her tongue brushed her lower lip. And her smile, with the mockery it contained, and the lasciviousness. I was able for her now, and that knowledge excited me.

"Fifteen grand would be an investment," I thought, "and a few grand for her to see a specialist and get back on her feet."
And I laughed out loud like a fucking heathen.

*- Kevin McDermott*

# GRACKLE

This art
can grasp me
from outside
and pull me
from this brush
through poison
and rash
in its hand
By first light
are the bones
of a grackle
withered
to the feelings
of its own
sound
through them
in the air
these bones
fly

*- Lawrence Bridges*

# THROWING OUT MY MOTHER'S SLIDES

No one wants them.
No one owns a slide projector.
Too many foreign landscapes and street scenes.
One-by-one I hold them up to the light,
hoping to see a face I might recognize.
Canyon bridges and floral fountains go,
and purchased views of ancient ruins.
Something about a village school
caught her eye and she committed it
to Ektachrome. I try to imagine her
there in the dust and heat so far from home.
I try to imagine her swaying her hips
with the belly dancers I'm looking at.
But she snapped the shot instead.

*- John Delaney*

# MOTHER, DAUGHTER

There was a time your eyes glowed red with anger, your mouth spitting spiteful shouts at me, your body burning with rancor, your arms unloving, pushing me away.

You were a bulldog that wouldn't let go of its bite, you pulled and pulled until cloth tore, flesh mangled, teeth sanguine.

You shoved and jabbed and hurt.

You were a hawk, your eyes sharp and cold, your beak strong and unforgiving. You dove from above, never missed your prey. Me.

There was a time I wondered, why me, why you.

My skin scarred, my soul bruised. And yet, we're tied by blood.

Only later and too late did I understand you cared but only learned the art of caring by attacking and burning.

I didn't know what ailed you, until you grew old and weak, your fire dimmed. The doctor shook his head, threw his hands in the air.

I had to know. You can't die on me like this, I said to you, me hating you, you hating me.
The fire in your belly continued to smolder, your eyes turned cloudy.

I took a kitchen knife, plunged into your entrails, and found all the pain in the world leaking into your organs, your nodes, running in your veins, seeping into your bones. The tumor you carried hidden in the cave of your soul, the metastasis of old wounds, sacrifice and grief encrypted into generational genes, mutations inherited from you to me. You let your past hurt and fester into the demon you couldn't expunge from the hollow of your throat even when you screamed incendiary insults. You couldn't excise that beast in you, or you'd have lost all the story of your life and all of you and me with you.

*Christine H. Chen*

# This is How You Pop

"DO IT THIS WAY," Chuck said, pulling in his cheeks, and then letting out a loud,

"Pop."

It was my third, first date in the last month. Each one its own shame. Each a terrible fall from a hope it might lead to someone to text between tedious tasks for my shit boss Marilyn or to watch Netflix with. This one had to work.

We found seats near the dance floor. "Take grape," Chuck said, and he thrust a Tootsie Pop towards me. "Go on, unwrap it." He waved his cherry lolly, like a conductor. EDM blared. I gripped my Cosmo and took a sip.

"See if you can make the pop sound," he said.

I surveyed the pop, so innocent in its purple wrapper.

"Be a sport," he said with a drop of impatience.

I unwrapped the pop, dunked it into my glass and stirred.

All around us were happy couples. Crammed around tiny tables. Wrapped up in each other's arms on the dance floor. A parade of high heels, bangles. More chiseled arms than at a sculpture garden.

I felt underdressed in my black jeans and lilac sweater. But I didn't want to look too eager, too decked out for this Chuck. This Chuck who looked so cute in his profile photo. This Chuck who wrote that he was a "Bicoastal finance exec, good dancer, makes great sushi rolls and loves rescue dogs." This Chuck in loafers, with no socks. He seemed so normal when we met for coffee last week. The kind of guy who wants to get a dog to raise with his girlfriend. But now I wasn't so sure. There was a red lollipop waving from his hand.

He stared at me. Sucked. Popped.

I considered another Sunday night with only Monday ahead of me. I reached for my drink, took a gulp, and then plonked the pop in my mouth. Vodka, cranberry, and grape lollipops. Who knew? Grape *was* my favorite. The sweetness melted on my tongue and slid down the back of my throat, warm and comforting. I felt the vodka heating up my arms, my neck loosened, my fingertips floated. "It's an amazing combination," I said. "Want to try?" He shook his head, no, and reached for his martini.

I sucked on the pop just as I used to as a kid.

"Come on, do it," Chuck said, almost begging, making the dreadful pop again.

There's something about disappointing people, especially people I don't know very well.

I held the Tootsie Pop between my cheeks, sucked and "*popped.*" It was a demure, dainty pop.
"No, like this." Chuck demonstrated, this time slowing down the "pop," his eyes trained on me, as if I was his student.
The *bat, bat, bat* pounded. My heart started to worry with quick noisy beats.
Did I even know if Chuck was his real name? Why would anyone want to be called Chuck?

I held my lollipop over the heat of the candle on the table, warming it, and then touched my tongue to the candy. It burned. I dropped it into my drink. He stared. It wasn't a friendly stare. His lip curled down as lowered his eyes on me, almost like a silent sneer.

"Try heating up yours," I said.

He ignored me. And the curl on his lip remained like a quiet threat. That was it. I'd had enough. I pushed back from the table and as I rose, he grabbed me. His face in my face. I popped my lollipop into my mouth with a hasty shove. But Chuck was not deterred. He took hold of my lollipop stick in his front teeth like a Tango dancer with a red rose and pulled. I leaned away. He tugged harder but I held on like a dog with a bone. Maybe I growled. The man had no chance.

I broke free and ran out the door. In the taxi, I bit down on the grape candy until it broke into shards, giving way to the soft, sweet chocolate inside.

*- Andrea Marcusa*

# Reading the Streets

~After "Mad Pepper" *

I found it while wandering Paris this morning. A flip on the typical aimless feet and made it three quarters through the city streets before I discovered treasure: *poverty's an ocean.* So much H20 but nary an ounce to drink. I sauntered many cobbled and un-cobbled roads, peered down every graffitied alley—past the hardware store with its junked out crew, the coffee shop, the parlor you stepped into for a haircut. Somewhere along the way you declared gender assignments for spices. Such a mad world.

I read the streets like tea leaves—find truth but no answers. I find freedom in the line *I had to pee* but become distracted by a key to an open door, retrace my steps and wonder which way to go for more. I'm too lazy to search for meaning in names and too easily distracted to make it to the end of the sidewalk. I like short poems and vanilla cream in my coffee. Vanilla is a stunningly complex and subtle spice. Most certainly female.

The streets could be cobbled with tanzanite or sapphire afire with the light of the sun and I'd still abandon these pursuits for the taste of sugar in my mouth. I'm a user wondering if I've earned the right to steal—rename each city I walk. With wry joy I pry green street signs with white letters off steel posts; brandish purple duct tape and cardboard—scent of permanent marker fresh in the air that surrounds me. Maybe I'm just high on it—walking, becoming & unbecoming, and the beauty of being anonymously in bloom.

It's Monday November 23rd. I've walked eight-thousand, four-hundred, eighty-eight steps so far. Some part of me is always quietly counting too.

- **Shyla Shehan**

* "Mad Pepper" is a poem by Eileen Myles, Paris Review Issue no. 102 (Spring 1987)

# THE CLEARING

IT ONLY TOOK TWO AND A HALF HOURS to drive from our home in Connecticut to my grandparents' up the Hudson in New York State, but we would never stay less than two nights, the distance we traveled seemed that great. I suppose it felt arduous because, after we crossed the river at Poughkeepsie, headed up 9-W past the Grand Union, the Bruderhof community, and Mother Cabrini's orphanage, we still had several trials of rural driving before we arrived at The Clearing.

My father would need to pull our red VW bug (one of any number with interchangeable parts for when they stopped working, which was often) over to the right at the stone church and sit with his left turn signal blinking until there was a brief lull in the impatient trucks flying by. He'd jam the reluctant car into gear and whip us across the highway and up a steep gravel hill that was the beginning of Burroughs Drive. This is when our travels truly began, into the woods, over the mountain, out of the world we had inhabited just moments before.

We'd grind past the fields and vineyards of Brother Barry's refuge for lonely men and scoop ourselves up toward the first bend, which might seem sharp if you didn't know what was coming later. A sweep of pasture showed itself below us, and in the far corner was the gnarled tree I would seek out years later when, in my early adulthood, I'd want to show my dying grandfather, my boyfriend, even the later owner of The Clearing, how its branches and leaves were actually hungry, huge poison ivy vines.

As a young child, I'd spot the tree's contour from a distance, not knowing that I might come later to regard it as one of the natural wonders of the world - why would I think of something so far away when there was the sound of straining tires pulling us up an ever-steepening slope toward the next bend and a sign that said "sound horn" and another that showed a serpent of turns ahead. The road had narrowed to one lane and we were meant to trust somehow that the driver of a vehicle barreling toward us from the other direction would hear the VW's anemic horn as we gingerly rounded that curve. No pullouts, no shoulder, just all the faith in the world.

I kept my eyes peeled for deer, chipmunks, the "Private Property Keep Out" signs that had always haunted me. After three more bends, the horn sounding more and more urgent, my breath being held more and more prayerfully, the neighbor's house came into view. It was green, square, on stilts, and the density of fir trees surrounding it made the scene into a treasure, something out of Primitivist paintings in which one expects to see disproportionate heads on two-dimensional animal bodies. The neighbor herself was a painter, although not of anything representational like trees or horses, so spotting her house was an entry into my grandparents' avant-garde art world as much as into a forested realm of mountain isolation.

Arrival at The Clearing was marked first by a view of the crumbling garage where my uncle had set up a makeshift sculpture studio since coming back to live with his parents and to dry out. The shingled house, with its endless screened porch, was encircled by trees that seemed to be leaning in to smell the tops of our heads. As we parked and unfolded ourselves from the car, the screen door spring creaked and twanged as my grandparents came out to greet us. My tall, loping grandfather Chan was quick with his chortling greeting while Grandma Betsy moved slower, more tentatively behind as though already considering what Buddha-like expression she might bestow upon us once we were inside and seated around her.

There were two main doors to the house (later three, after Chan designed and built an expansive addition) but we always entered through the long porch which seemed in itself to be an extension of the woods and the road and the slopes and the curves. This was the final tunnel into something that wasn't quite the past, but certainly wasn't anything like the present we had left behind in Connecticut. On one side of the porch was a table where we'd eat our meals, with food handed out through a window from the kitchen, and we'd look out into a darkness of trees, watching fireflies building up their light, listening as owls found their night voices.

On the porch's long side, lined with Adirondack chairs, our view was framed by grasping branches as we would look down the sharp slope to a slice of the Hudson. It was the very spot on the river where the water turned from brackish to fresh, so the boats would dock there to empty out before continuing on their passage north. Betsy kept a guestbook and a pair of binoculars on the porch railing and would write down the names of the boats, their arrival and departure times, anything else of interest. This practice, along with her record of the various birds who would visit the nearer vegetation, were the poetic rituals of my grandmother's resignation to country life after years in Chicago and New York City. To me as a child, these weren't things to be done out of pleasure, or boredom, or grief, they were just things to be done at The Clearing by an aging occupant finding her way toward being one with her quiet environment.

On many visits, we walked a mile up the road as it became more like a deer path and led farther into another place. Its terminus was Slabsides, the decomposing cabin of naturalist John Burroughs, for whom the mountain and road were named. There was a society of volunteers who maintained the property and opened it to visitors by appointment so that we might view the relics of Burroughs' work and world amidst the smell of damp wood, moss, and mushrooms.

Slabsides is where I first became aware that houses are capsules of their most tenacious residents' lives, all the more when they're protected and hidden by trees and rugged terrain. As we walked back down the road to The Clearing, some part of me sensed that my grandparents' house was becoming such a capsule, but I knew so little of what it contained. As my grandfather planned and executed his masterpiece of an expansion, building on his years working for Frank Lloyd Wright, I saw only the physical features as they evolved: the monumental windows overlooking the river, the little greenhouse for Betsy's African violets, the study Chan lovingly designed for her to face out onto bushes visited by song birds, the separate loft space for my uncle, and the floor's trap door with a pulley meant to heave up stone and tree stumps for chiseling.

Only gradually did I become aware of everything else contained in those spaces, surrounded by those timeless woods: Betsy's decay through depression and osteoporosis, the wilted and browning leaves of plants in the greenhouse, Chan's depletion from cancer and professional disappointments, the bitter tension between my uncle and his father, how Chan was ridiculed by his kin when all he produced from the pulley and its weighty material were stools and cartoonish animal heads, and how one year my sister and I were stowed at The Clearing for a few days as my mother aborted a baby she couldn't bring herself to raise. The tortuous road, the concealing conifers, the steep slopes weren't only splendor; they could just as easily be agents of alienation, loss of access to the world outside and below.

The tree standing so twisted and picturesque in the corner of the field – I suppose, when I finally saw it up close, that I became intoxicated by its grotesqueness, by something horrifying in the fact that it wasn't living but, rather, was being consumed by a throbbing, toxic vine whose shiny leaves threatened from afar, if you knew what you were looking at.

The sadness and poverty of the men working on Brother Barry's farm, being guided away from addiction and self-destruction by a community of Episcopal monks, themselves straining against sadness and poverty. My grandfather's final social action was to protest the sale of the farm to developers. It sold nonetheless.

And at the very base of Burroughs Drive, facing away from the gravel that wound into the forested maw, where we would wait, peering across 9-W while trying to pull out between the racing trucks, is the stone church where Betsy asked to be taken on a growing number of Sundays as she was able to do less and less.

A minister's daughter from Missouri, she had journeyed into Communist circles, written letters to her not-yet-husband about the wonders of sex, moved around the country to realize one ideal of alternative education after another, exposed the wickedness of Blackwell's Island in her social work research, and had all but shouted "Such beautiful naked bodies!" from her wheelchair as she and I left a Swedish film festival in Rhinebeck.

The Clearing's sedentary solitude had brought her back to church, down the mountain, out of the woods, to its rites, its regularity. And when she died in her sleep, it was Chan who, in a suit and tie not worn in decades, came out from the shelter of fir-tree overhang and recklessly drove past the neighbor painter's house, the "keep out" signs, the deer and the chipmunks, honking his horn better-late-than-never coming around first one, then a second, then a third bend, past an ivy-choked tree standing solitary in a fallow field, past a construction site of long-shuttered and soon-to-be-demolished farm buildings. He made it across the highway in one piece and carried his lanky frame into the cold little sanctuary where this minister's son from Illinois, this free-thinking artist with no sense of time and no patience for limits, knelt and took communion in her memory before heading back up the hill to live, alone, a short while longer among the trees.

A child's unquestioning eyes, the immediacy of her sensations, and the simplicity of her experience collude to keep a mountain magical, to make the chill of a forest's damp shade transporting even if slightly uncomfortable, and to allow the activity of the river below to seem not so far away because it was well within our view.

Only upon leaving, close to the bottom of the mountain, below the wood's edge, and a ways into my adolescence, did the mixed symbols and messages begin to show themselves so that I began to understand The Clearing as a capsule not only of sweetness and quiet, but of sorrow and loss.


*- Vivian Montgomery*

SUBMISSIONS FOR THE ANNUAL
# JULIA DARLING MEMORIAL
# POETRY PRIZE
WINNER RECEIVES $1200. 2ND PLACE $100
SUBMISSIONS OPEN: **May 1**
SUBMISSIONS CLOSE: **Midnight August 20**

*The Julia Darling Memorial Poetry Prize winner will be published in The Ocotillo Review Volume 7.1*

_All entrants will receive a copy of the journal and be considered for publication.

_Submit 1-3 poems in a single document per entry. Begin each poem on a separate page. Limit poems to 65 lines including title and spaces. Entries should not exceed 10 pages.

_There is a $20.00 fee per entry. Poets may submit multiple entries by paying additional entry fees.

_Do not put your name or other identifying info on the document or in the submission title.

_We welcome the expression of diverse voices, diverse cultures - including poems partly or entirely in languages other than English. Please include an English translation.

_No previously published poems - print or online - will be accepted. This includes poems posted on personal websites or social network pages or groups.

_We will accept simultaneous submissions for the Julia Darling Memorial Poetry Prize with the understanding that any poem published elsewhere will be withdrawn immediately.

More info available at
**www.kallistogaiapress**

# CONTRIBUTORS

C B Anderson   cbanderson.net
John Bradley   spdbooks.org/Products/9781880834909
Lawrence Bridges  en.wikipedia.org/wiki/Lawrence_Bridges
Craig Cotter   www.craigcotter.com
John Delaney   www.johnmdelaney.com/
David Desjardins   www.linkedin.com/in/desjardinsdavid/
Dianne Dugaw   www.amazon.com/Dianne-Dugaw
Joanne Durham   www.joannedurham.com
Steven Fromm
Ray Gonzalez   cla.umn.edu/about/directory/profile/gonza049
Dr. Alex Van Huynh
Lorraine Jeffery  www.amazon.com/Lorraine-Jeffery
Kaitlin Kan
Candice Kelsey   www.candicemkelseypoet.com
Karen Lethlean penfactor.com/competition/pub/1464233418857
Stephen Lyons   muckrack.com/lyonssj55/articles
Andrea Marcusa   andreamarcusa.com
Kevin McDermott   https://littleisland.ie/authors/kevin-mcdermott/
Vivian Montgomery vivianmontgomery.org/index.html
Kurt Olsson  poets.org/poet/kurt-s-olsson
Harry Palacio  linkedin.com/in/harry-palacio-57340331/
Shannon Perri   www.shannonperri.com
M. Ann Reed
Claire Scott  clairescottpoet.com/
Robin Scofield  www.robinscofield.com/
Frank Scozzari  http://frankscozzari.com/index.html
Shyla Shehan   shylashehan.com
James Stemmle
Elizabeth Vrenios  linkedin.com/in/elizabeth-vrenios-8a8643b/
William Waters
Richard Weaver  theamericanjournalofpoetry.com/v7-weaver.html
Wyatt Welch  http://wyattwelch.org/